Quick and Easy 5-Ingredient Cookbook

Quick and Easy 5-Ingredient Cookbook

30-MINUTE RECIPES TO GET STARTED IN THE KITCHEN

Eileen Kelly

Photography by Elysa Weitala

ROCKRIDGE PRESS

For general information on our other products and services or to obtain technical support, please contact our Customer Care Department within the United States at (866) 744-2665, or outside the United States at (510) 253-0500.

Rockridge Press publishes its books in a variety of electronic and print formats. Some content that appears in print may not be available in electronic books, and vice versa.

Interior and Cover Designer: John Clifford
Art Producer: Sara Feinstein
Editor: Laura Apperson
Production Editor: Mia Moran

Photography © 2020 Elysa Weitala. Food styling by Victoria Woollard

Author photo courtesy of © Shannon Lee

ISBN: Print 978-1-64611-907-3 | eBook 978-1-64611-908-0

R0

Thank you to my hubs,
Matthew, and my kids—the loves of
my life—Matt, Mairead, Aidan, and
Deirdre, for being my forever
taste testers! XO

Contents

Introduction

Welcome to the *Quick and Easy 5-Ingredient Cookbook*! Whether you are an experienced home cook or a newbie, you'll find everything you need to enjoy great food in 30 minutes. Even better, you'll be using simple, familiar pantry items for easy preparation—and you probably have most of them in your kitchen already.

I know a lot of non-cooks and people who are too busy to cook. My oldest daughter loves to eat, but for her, cooking is a challenge. My best friend works long hours, and when she gets home, she doesn't want to be in the kitchen for hours. This book is for them and for anyone who is looking for quick and easy meals that are delicious.

As a full-time writer, taxi driver, clothes-washer, bed-maker, and head chef of a family of six, I'm always swamped. I use the recipes in this book all the time. And if my daughter can make every one of these recipes with ease, you can, too!

This cookbook includes recipes for breakfast, lunch, dinner, and dessert that contain five ingredients or less, so you can enjoy incredible meals all day. And because the recipes can be prepared in 30 minutes or less, enjoying a home-cooked meal is not only delicious, satisfying, and cost effective, it's just minutes away.

Cooking at home is healthier and easier than takeout because you decide what ingredients to buy. Your juicy homemade burger includes the exact toppings you want without any preservatives, *and* it will be on your table faster than you can get to a restaurant. Amp up the flavor with a seasoning blend, and you'll lose interest in fast-food burgers.

Although this is a five-ingredient cookbook, there are a few basic ingredients that don't count as one of the five:

- nonstick cooking spray
- butter
- olive oil
- pepper
- salt
- water

The DIY spice blends in chapter 9 that include salt and pepper as a base will be terrific time-savers for adding flavor to food. Mix these up ahead of time and store them in small jars so they are ready to use. Once you get the hang of making the seasoning blends in this book, try creating your own. No need to buy expensive seasoning blends.

Let's create some beautiful, delicious meals together. I'm getting hungry already!

Dinner in a Flash

Let's get acquainted in the kitchen, starting with the tools you'll need to make an enticing meal in 30 minutes or less. With just a few essentials, some amazing spices, pantry items, and a well-stocked refrigerator, you'll be well on your way to deliciousness. You'll be thrilled about the amount of money you save by dining in. Plus, cooking at home will enhance your culinary skills and open up your palate to new flavors and dishes. Open this book, pick a recipe, and say goodbye to takeout. You're on your way to a tasty meal.

< From top, clockwise: Mom's Homemade Tomato Soup, page 24; Balsamic-and-Honey-Glazed Salmon, page 57; Roasted Lemon Asparagus, page 85

Get Ready for Simple, Delicious Meals

With just a little organization, you'll be ready to make every recipe in this book. Grow your confidence and expand your creativity by trying the variations of ingredients and spice blends. As you create delicious, time-saving, and budget-friendly recipes every day, you'll become more self-assured in the kitchen.

THE BENEFITS OF QUICK AND EASY

As you're deciding where to begin, be sure to stock your kitchen and equip yourself with the essentials that you'll need to make these quick and easy recipes. Chances are you already have most of the staples and basic tools.

My mantra for this book is: 5 ingredients or less plus 30 minutes equals 100 percent deliciousness. I'm excited to share with you some of the reasons why I love this concept.

You will feel better after a home-cooked meal. You don't always know what you're getting when you eat out, but when you cook at home, you know what the ingredients are, and you can choose healthy options.

You will save money. No more waiting in drive-through lines or for pizza delivery and worrying if you have enough cash.

Five ingredients equals simplicity. Using just a few high-quality ingredients keeps your meals simple yet loaded with flavor. No need to settle for soggy fries or greasy pizza.

It's quick and easy. You don't need hours in the kitchen to enjoy delicious food. In less time than it takes to pick up a fast-food meal, you can make your own homemade creations.

Home-cooked is better than frozen. Enjoying a preservative-free, home-cooked meal is not only cost effective, it's much healthier than frozen prepackaged meals. You can make a hearty pot of soup and a fresh salad, a delicious burger, a mouthwatering pork tenderloin, or even the ever-popular chicken tenders in less than 30 minutes.

EFFICIENT GROCERY SHOPPING

I don't mind spending time in the grocery store, but I know it isn't on the top of everyone's list of places to be! To help you shop more efficiently, spend less, and save time, I've compiled a cheat sheet of my top tricks for efficient grocery shopping.

Never, ever go grocery shopping hungry. This tip includes online shopping as well. You're much less likely to binge-buy on a full tummy.

Be sure to meal plan. It takes just a few minutes to plan what you want to eat for the week and create a grocery list. Stick to the list and don't waiver. It's easier to stay on budget when you stick to the list.

Pay attention to the deals of the week. Grocery stores always offer bargains, so plan your weekly menu around them. If chicken is on sale, make chicken that week.

Organize your shopping list according to the store's aisles. If you don't like wasting time at the grocery store, an organized list will get you through quickly and efficiently.

Shop online. Save time by ordering your groceries online and picking them up at the store. Ordering your groceries online will also keep you from spontaneously adding things that you really don't need.

Shop early. If you shop at the store, the earlier you go, the fewer shoppers will be there, which will help you get out quickly.

Buy meat and poultry in bulk. Break down large packages of meat, divide them into freezer-safe resealable bags, and store them in the freezer. Defrost as needed. You can also buy canned beans and soup stocks in bulk. They can stay on the shelf for quite a while.

Make double batches of soups, pesto, or baked chicken. Eat one batch that evening and freeze the second batch. You'll always have something in the freezer that can defrost quickly on those nights when you really have no time at all to cook.

EXPERT COOKING TIPS

Becoming an expert in the kitchen happens gradually. As you learn how to organize and plan your meals, you'll build confidence and be more efficient in the kitchen. Just keep at it!

Throughout the book, I share tips and tricks to help you succeed in the kitchen. Here are a few to get you started:

1. **Read the recipe twice.** Do this before beginning the cooking process to make sure you understand the steps. Check that you have the necessary ingredients before you begin cooking.

2. **Invest in a good knife.** Purchase a good-quality knife set if your budget allows. Be sure to keep your knives sharp. There's nothing worse than trying to use dull knives to cut meat or veggies. A knife sharpener is a good tool if you want to sharpen your knives yourself. There are many affordable varieties that do a wonderful job of sharpening knives, and they are very easy to use. Take good care of your knives. Hand wash them instead of placing them in the dishwasher, which can scratch and dull them. Invest in a knife rack, block, or magnetic wall strip, which will keep the knives stored properly.

3. **Practice *mise en place*.** This French term, used often by professional chefs, simply means to prepare all the ingredients before you begin cooking. Chop and dice meat and veggies and measure out spices. As you finish working with a tool or dish, put it in the sink or dishwasher. Have a cloth ready for quickly cleaning spills and tidying up as the food is cooking.

4. **Use delicious spice blends.** You will be amazed at how much flavor these blends will add to your food. It may sound overwhelming to make your own spice blend, but it is really quite simple. I have included some of my favorites in chapter 9 (page 95). My wish is that you make them and use them throughout the book. Once you're comfortable making the blends in this book, use them to create new recipes. Then get courageous and make your own blends.

5. **Never add ingredients to a cold pan.** Let the pan warm, then hold your hand about six inches above it. If you feel warmth, begin cooking. Warming the pan before cooking will help you avoid making greasy or soggy food. But remember, for safety's sake, never walk away from a pan that's warming on the stove.

6. **Use time wisely.** While pasta is cooking, make a sauce. If chicken is baking, cook some veggies. If you stay organized, you stay efficient. If you are new to the kitchen, keep a task list and check off each completed item as you go.

7. **Follow the heating instructions.** If the recipe states to cook your chicken over medium heat, turning the heat to high won't make it cook faster. Instead, the meat will burn on the outside while remaining raw on the inside.

8. **Ensure protein is dry.** When cooking meat, poultry, fish, or tofu, it should not be wet when you add it to a sauté pan. Blot the exterior of the food with a paper towel. Drying the protein before cooking it ensures a good sear on its exterior, which is what seals the flavor inside.

9. **Follow the recipe, especially if you're a new chef.** Make the recipe a few times. Once you're comfortable with the written version, you can get a bit creative and swap out some of the ingredients.

LIGHTNING-QUICK CLEANUP

Cleanup is the part of cooking we all dread. Trust me, it doesn't have to be a big chore. Grab your smartphone or another device and blast your favorite song. Then follow these tips for quick cleanup!

1. Keep your trash can close by for quick disposal of waste.

2. Line baking pans with aluminum foil for easy cleanup. Check out the Foil Packet Fish Fillets and Tomatoes (page 56) for an example of an easy, delicious recipe that uses foil.

3. For sheet pan meals, line the pan with parchment paper to make cleaning simple.

4. Keep your workspace tidy. It is so important to practice *mise en place* and keep a tidy workspace as you cook. Have a towel nearby or in your apron to take care of little spills before they turn into big messes.

5. If your kitchen has a dishwasher, put the dirty dishes in as you cook. If you have a dirty pan or pot that needs an extra-long cleaning, soak it while you finish cooking.

6. Did your family enjoy their mouthwatering meal? Then enlist their help for cleanup. Many hands make fast work, and whoever puts things away the quickest and neatest can get a hug.

Keeping a Stocked Kitchen

To create a great meal, it really helps to have the proper equipment and a well-stocked pantry. The following lists show you what is essential and what's nice to have if you have the time and money to get the items. But remember, with the basics, you can make every recipe in this book.

TIME-SAVING EQUIPMENT

The following kitchen staples will help you be successful in the kitchen. These items are must-haves that will save you the most time, followed by more basic must-haves and nice-to-have items.

Cutting board: Invest in a sturdy cutting board to protect your countertops while you efficiently cut ingredients. Wood, plastic, and bamboo are the most common types. If you're able, use separate boards for meat and veggies.

Grater: Graters come in many sizes, and they will make shredding and grating cheese easy. They are affordable and a must for speed.

Juicers: Manual juicers are not expensive, and they are great tools for extracting juice quickly from fruits. You can also buy electronic juicers.

Knife set: A good set of knives is important for easy cutting and dicing. If you can only choose one knife, start with a sturdy chef's knife and add other knives as your skills grow.

Strainer: A fine mesh strainer makes it easy to drain beans, tomatoes, and pasta and to strain seeds from lemons.

Utensils: Wooden spoons, ladles, kitchen scissors, spatulas, a slotted spoon, a vegetable peeler, and tongs are important to have an easy cooking experience.

Whisk: A whisk is great for blending eggs to make them light and fluffy. Use it for baking as well.

Must-Haves

Baking dish: A 9-by-13-inch baking dish is a great basic size.

Bowls: Start with a set of three—small, medium, and large.

Can opener: Basic handheld openers are inexpensive. There are also electric openers that won't break the bank.

Colander: Use this tool to drain pasta, beans, and excess liquid from canned foods.

Measuring cups and spoons: These tools ensure correct measurements of your ingredients.

Muffin tin: Start with a 12-cup tin and add others if you make muffins frequently.

Saucepan: A 3-quart pan is a fundamental tool to make sauces.

Sheet pan: Every kitchen should be equipped with at least one 9-by-13-inch sheet pan.

Skillet: A 10-inch nonstick skillet is an essential tool for making omelets and for sautéing meats and vegetables.

Stockpot: An 8-quart stockpot is a good starter pot to make soups, stocks, and chilis.

Nice-to-Haves

Air fryer: This tool is great for frying food without oil.

Blender: This appliance is perfect for making smoothies or other condiments, like pesto.

Electric pressure cooker: Use this device to quickly cook food under steam pressure.

Food processor: This appliance makes dicing, chopping, and combining ingredients easy.

Immersion blender: Personally, I can't live without my immersion blender, as it easily purées soups directly in a stockpot or slow cooker.

Mini-chopper: This tool is great for quickly chopping veggies.

Salad spinner: Another of my favorite tools, a salad spinner lets you quickly clean fresh greens.

Slow cooker: Food cooks long and slow in this appliance. Add ingredients in the morning and come home to a fully cooked dinner. A slow cooker is a fantastic addition to any kitchen.

Stand mixer: This tool is very useful for mixing cookie doughs and cake batters.

STAPLE INGREDIENTS

All the recipes in this book are quick, but having your shelves and refrigerator fully stocked makes preparation much easier.

In the Refrigerator

Butter: Use butter in desserts and for sautéing and adding flavor to foods. Unless otherwise noted, the recipes in this book call for unsalted butter. Butter does not count as one of the five ingredients in the recipes.

Cheese: Both hard and soft cheeses, such as Parmesan and Cheddar, add flavor and depth to just about any recipe.

Dijon mustard: A must-have for enhancing the flavor of salad dressings and marinades.

Herbs: Fresh herbs enhance flavor and bring freshness to food, although in a pinch, dried herbs are fine.

Eggs: You'll use eggs for baking and for making easy, delicious breakfasts and quick dinners.

Fruit: Lemons and limes infuse salad dressings and sauces with a wonderfully tangy flavor. Keep a variety of your favorite fruits, like berries, apples, and bananas, on hand for snacking and adding to your favorite recipes.

Garlic: This ingredient really enhances so many recipes. You can buy minced garlic in a jar, but I think fresh garlic makes the best flavor enhancer.

Milk: Whether you prefer whole, low-fat, skim, or nut milk, keep one or more varieties on hand for egg recipes and for making breaded poultry and pork dishes.

Vegetables: Keep a variety of your favorite fresh vegetables on hand for easy side dishes and salad enhancers.

In the Freezer

Seafood: Keep a supply of frozen shrimp and white fish in the freezer. They defrost quickly and make cost-effective meals.

Meat and poultry: When there's a sale, purchase your meats in bulk. Store in freezer-safe storage bags for future meals.

Vegetables: Keep a few favorite frozen vegetables in the freezer for soups, quick side dishes, and stir-fry recipes. They can make for an easy dinner.

In the Pantry

Black pepper: This seasoning doesn't count as one of the five ingredients in these recipes. It's considered a staple and adds flavor to just about any recipe.

Broths: Canned beef, chicken, and vegetable broths are essential for soups and sauces. You can freeze leftover broth in an airtight container for up to four months.

Herbs: Every kitchen should have a selection of dried spices. Some basics to begin with include parsley, basil, thyme, oregano, garlic powder, and onion powder.

Kosher salt and iodized salt: Salt doesn't count as one of the five ingredients. It enhances any recipe and is also used in baking.

Nonstick cooking spray: This noncaloric spray creates a nonstick surface for sautéing. It doesn't count as one of the five ingredients.

Olive oil: Use this oil for sautéing, salad dressings, and marinades. Olive oil doesn't count as one of the five ingredients.

Pasta: For easy dinners, keep a variety of dry pastas on your shelves. Common types include spaghetti, elbow, and penne.

Vinegars: A variety of vinegars are vital for making salad dressings, sauces, and marinades. A few common ones to start with include red wine, balsamic, and apple cider vinegar.

KEEPING FOOD FRESH

Food waste is one of the most important things to avoid in the kitchen. Here are some simple ways to use all the food in your refrigerator and prevent food from going bad.

1. **If you can't use a food, freeze it for later use.** When freezing food, take care to store the item correctly in an airtight, freezer-safe container. Label the container with the name of the ingredients and the date it was frozen.

2. **Keep homemade spices in covered, labeled Mason jars.** Try the spice blends in chapter 9. They make everything taste better. Spices and blends will stay fresh for up to six months.

3. **Store produce properly:**
   - Potatoes and onions are best stored in a cool, dark pantry, not in the refrigerator.
   - Tomatoes should be stored at room temperature, as they go bad faster in the refrigerator.
   - If your salad greens are going limp, drop them in ice cold water to perk up the leaves.
   - Keep herbs in a glass of water on a windowsill to keep them fresh longer.

4. **Defrost meat in the refrigerator rather than on the counter.** Simply put a frozen package of meat in the refrigerator before you go to bed and by the time you are ready to cook the next day, it should be defrosted.

Here is a guide for storing various foods in the refrigerator and freezer, according to the USDA.

FOOD	REFRIGERATOR	FREEZER
Chicken, raw	1–2 days	3–4 months
Eggs, cooked and omelets	3–4 days	2 months
Fish, raw	1 day	2–3 months
Ground beef and pork, raw	1–2 days	3–4 months
Pesto, homemade	5–6 days	6 months
Salads	3–5 days	Doesn't freeze well
Soup, leftover	3–4 days	2–3 months

How to Use This Book

In this book, the five or less primary ingredients in each recipe have been bolded. Remember that nonstick cooking spray, butter, olive oil, pepper, salt, and water do not count toward the five main ingredients. Each chapter starts with a master recipe, which include variations and often use seasoning blends from chapter 9. The seasoning blends are versatile and can be used on meat, poultry, veggies, and in sauces.

Use the shopping tips from Efficient Grocery Shopping (page 3) to stay on target by keeping your shopping trips short and your pantry and refrigerator stocked. Don't forget to create your shopping list, plan ahead for one week of meals, and check your store for sales to stock up on items you use regularly.

Keep an eye out for these useful tips throughout the book:

Addition Tip: These are five-ingredient recipes. If you have a little extra time, when appropriate, there will be suggestions of ingredients to add to the recipe.

Cooking Tip: This tip tells you how to keep the cooking process flowing to ensure success.

Shortcut: Throughout the book, I will share tips to make recipes even quicker and easier.

Storage Tip: This tip will tell you how long to refrigerate or freeze the recipe.

Substitution Tip: Cooking is very forgiving. If you don't have or don't like an ingredient, there is always an option for substitution.

Variation Tip: Many of the recipes include variations, which will make this cookbook useful for a long time.

Some recipes will include the following labels:

One-Pan or One-Pot: One cooking vessel will be needed to make this recipe.

Sheet Pan: The recipe will be made on a baking sheet or sheet pan.

No-Cook: The recipe will not need to be cooked or baked.

Freezer-Friendly: Freezer-friendly recipes will have instructions for freezing, defrosting, and reheating. The instructions will also say how long the food can be kept in the freezer.

Dairy-Free

Gluten-Free

Nut-Free

Be sure to check any packaged ingredients for allergen info, as some commonly used items may contain traces of dairy, gluten, or nuts.

Breakfasts

< Sheet Pan French Toast, page 20

My Favorite Omelet

SERVES 1 / PREP TIME: 5 MINUTES / COOK TIME: 5 MINUTES

Once you know how to make a basic omelet, you'll discover its versatility. Whether you enjoy them for breakfast, lunch, or a late-night snack, all you need to do to create a new dish with completely different flavors is switch out a few ingredients and add some others. I've included a few variations—consider them a jumping-off point to create your own one-of-a-kind omelet. I like to serve my omelet with Maple-Turkey Breakfast Patties (page 16), though a couple slices of crisp bacon on the side is also nice.

2 large eggs

1 teaspoon cold water

¼ teaspoon salt

¼ teaspoon freshly ground black pepper

1 teaspoon butter

¼ cup shredded Cheddar cheese

1. Heat an 8-inch skillet over medium heat.
2. In a medium mixing bowl, whisk together the eggs, water, salt, and pepper until well blended.
3. Melt the butter in the skillet and tilt the pan to spread it out evenly. Pour the eggs into the pan and cook, using a wooden spoon to lift the edges of the eggs as they set so the liquid egg goes beneath the cooked egg, about 1 minute.
4. Sprinkle the cheese on half of the omelet.
5. Using a spatula, fold the other side over the cheese, slide the omelet onto a plate, and serve.

Per Serving: Calories: 399; Total fat: 31g; Sodium: 1,084mg; Carbohydrates: 2g; Fiber: <1g; Sugar: <1g; Protein: 25g

VARIATIONS

Mexican

Add ½ teaspoon of Taco Seasoning Mix (page 97) when you whisk the eggs, water, salt, and pepper. Melt the butter, add 1 tablespoon of chopped bell peppers, and sauté about 2 minutes until softened. Set the peppers aside. Cook the eggs as instructed. Instead of Cheddar, sprinkle ¼ cup of Colby jack, 1 tablespoon of salsa, and the peppers over one half of the omelet. Fold and serve with chopped cilantro and chopped tomatoes.

Per Serving: Calories: 423; Total fat: 32g; Sodium: 1,155mg; Carbohydrates: 8g; Fiber: 1g; Sugar: 3g; Protein: 26g

Italian Herb, Tomato, and Mozzarella

Add ½ teaspoon of Italian Herb Seasoning Mix (page 97) when you whisk together the eggs, water, salt, and pepper. Cook as instructed. Instead of Cheddar cheese, sprinkle 2 teaspoons of chopped tomato and ¼ cup of shredded mozzarella over one half of the omelet. Fold and serve with chopped basil and additional chopped tomatoes, if desired.

Per Serving: Calories: 346; Total fat: 24g; Sodium: 1,107mg; Carbohydrates: 7g; Fiber: 1g; Sugar: <1g; Protein: 27g

Cajun Ham and Spicy Jack Cheese

Add ½ teaspoon of Cajun Seasoning Mix (page 97) when you whisk the eggs, water, salt, and pepper. Melt the butter, add 2 ounces of diced ham to the skillet, and sauté about 1 minute until warm. Set the ham aside. Cook the eggs. Instead of Cheddar, sprinkle the ham and ¼ cup of pepper jack over one half of the omelet. Fold and serve.

Per Serving: Calories: 469; Total fat: 33g; Sodium: 1,804mg; Carbohydrates: 6g; Fiber: <1g; Sugar: 3g; Protein: 36g

Bacon, Avocado, and Cheddar

Add ½ teaspoon of Seasoned Salt (page 96) when you whisk the eggs, water, salt, and pepper. Cook as instructed. Sprinkle the Cheddar, ¼ cup of cooked bacon, and one half of a chopped avocado over half of the omelet. Fold and serve with chopped tomatoes.

Per Serving: Calories: 633; Total fat: 52g; Sodium: 1,486mg; Carbohydrates: 10g; Fiber: 6g; Sugar: 1g; Protein: 31g

Vegetable and Cheese

Whisk the eggs, water, salt, and pepper and melt the butter. Add ¼ cup of your vegetable of choice (chopped broccoli, mushrooms, spinach, or diced peppers) and sauté 1 to 2 minutes until softened. Set the vegetables aside. Cook the eggs. Sprinkle your choice of cheese (crumbled feta, shredded Gruyère, or shredded Swiss) over half of the omelet. Fold and serve.

Per Serving (with broccoli and feta cheese): Calories: 344; Total fat: 26g; Sodium: 1,372mg; Carbohydrates: 6g; Fiber: 2g; Sugar: 4g; Protein: 22g

Maple-Turkey Breakfast Patties

SERVES 4 / PREP TIME: 5 MINUTES / COOK TIME: 15 MINUTES

After you make these tasty treats, you'll never want a store-bought patty again. These breakfast patties are full of flavor from the spices and the maple syrup, which adds a warm sweetness that blends with the spices and turkey. Ground chicken or pork can be used instead of turkey.

1 pound ground turkey

1 teaspoon Seasoned Salt (page 96)

1 teaspoon maple syrup

1 teaspoon dried thyme

½ teaspoon cayenne pepper (optional)

Nonstick cooking spray

1. In a medium bowl, combine the ground turkey, seasoned salt, maple syrup, thyme, and cayenne (if using). Form the mixture into 4 patties.
2. Heat a skillet over medium heat. Spray with nonstick cooking spray.
3. Add the patties and cook until browned, about 6 minutes. Flip and continue to cook until cooked through, 6 to 7 minutes.

Storage Tip: To freeze the sausage patties, stack them between sheets of wax paper and place them in a resealable, freezer-safe bag. To use, defrost in the refrigerator overnight. Wrap the sausages in aluminum foil and bake for 10 minutes in a 375°F oven. I often make a double batch and freeze them, so I'll always have them ready.

Cooking Tip: Don't disturb the patty while it's cooking. Let it brown and flip it only when you are sure it's ready.

Per Serving: Calories: 168; Total fat: 8g; Sodium: 282mg; Carbohydrates: 2g; Fiber: <1g; Sugar: 1g; Protein: 22g

VARIATION

Sausage, Egg, and Cheese Sandwich

Toast an English muffin and place it on a plate. Place 1 slice of American cheese on one half of the English muffin. Melt 1 teaspoon of butter in a small skillet over medium heat. Add 1 cooked breakfast patty and cook for 2 minutes, then flip and cook for an additional 1 minute. Place the sausage on the cheese-covered English muffin. In the same skillet, crack 1 egg into the pan and cook for about 5 minutes. Season with salt and pepper to taste. Flip the egg over and cook for an additional 1 minute. Place the egg on the sausage and top with the remaining half of the English muffin. Serve warm.

Per Serving: Calories: 492; Total fat: 24g; Sodium: 865mg; Carbohydrates: 29g; Fiber: 1g; Sugar: 3g; Protein: 37g

Western Egg Breakfast Muffins

SERVES 4 / PREP TIME: 5 MINUTES / COOK TIME: 20 MINUTES

I love egg muffins because I can take them anywhere. And you can use your favorite veggies to personalize your muffin. These muffins are perfect make-and-take delights that are full of healthy ingredients for an energizing treat. Make a double batch, freeze them, and you'll always have a satisfying breakfast at the ready.

Nonstick cooking spray

8 eggs

6 ounces diced ham

1 red bell pepper, seeded and chopped

½ cup shredded Cheddar cheese

Salt

Freshly ground black pepper

1. Preheat the oven to 350°F. Spray a 6-cup muffin tin with nonstick spray. Set aside.
2. In a large bowl, whisk together the eggs, 1 teaspoon of water, ham, bell pepper, and Cheddar cheese. Season with salt and pepper.
3. Pour the egg mixture into the muffin tins and bake for 20 minutes. Transfer to a wire rack and let cool before removing from the muffin tins. Repeat as needed with any remaining egg mixture. Serve warm.

Storage Tip: The muffins can be stored in the refrigerator for up to 3 days or frozen in a freezer-safe bag for up to 2 months. To reheat, defrost in the refrigerator overnight. Preheat the oven to 350°F, wrap the muffins in aluminum foil, place on a baking sheet, and heat for 10 minutes until warm.

Cooking Tip: The recipe makes 8 egg muffins made in standard-size muffin tins. A 6-cup muffin tin is used in this recipe. If using a 12-cup muffin tin, make all the egg muffins at one time.

Per Serving (2 muffins): Calories: 284; Total fat: 19g; Sodium: 792mg; Carbohydrates: 4g; Fiber: 1g; Sugar: <1g; Protein: 23g

VARIATION

Pesto, Tomato, and Mozzarella Egg Muffins

Instead of using ham and bell pepper, add 1 teaspoon of Nut-Free Basil Pesto (page 98), ½ teaspoon of Italian Herb Seasoning Mix (page 97), and instead of the Cheddar, add 2 teaspoons of shredded mozzarella to the egg mixture. Follow the rest of the recipe as instructed.

Per Serving: Calories: 154; Total fat: 10g; Sodium: 263mg; Carbohydrates: 1g; Fiber: 0g; Sugar: <1g; Protein: 13g

Sheet Pan French Toast

SERVES 4 / PREP TIME: 10 MINUTES / COOK TIME: 15 TO 20 MINUTES

French toast is a great way to start the day, but who wants to stand in front of a griddle all morning? Making it on a sheet pan really speeds up the process so everyone can enjoy a hearty, comfort-filled breakfast at the same time. You can make a large batch and freeze the slices so you'll have them on hand for later.

Nonstick cooking spray

2 eggs

½ cup milk

1 teaspoon vanilla extract

½ teaspoon ground cinnamon

8 slices of brioche bread or challah bread

OPTIONAL TOPPINGS:

Maple syrup

Fresh fruit, such as sliced bananas, strawberries, or blueberries

Powdered sugar

1. Preheat the oven to 375°F. Spray a large baking sheet with the nonstick cooking spray.

2. In a shallow bowl, whisk together the eggs, milk, vanilla, and cinnamon.

3. Dip a slice of bread into the egg mixture, turning to coat both sides. Let the excess egg mixture drip back into the bowl. Place the egg-dipped bread onto the baking sheet. Repeat with the remaining bread slices.

4. Bake for 10 minutes. Remove the tray from the oven and flip each slice of bread. If needed, spray the pan with more nonstick cooking spray. Bake for another 5 to 6 minutes, until crispy and golden brown.

5. Serve hot with optional toppings (if using) and enjoy.

Storage Tip: To freeze, place the French toast slices on a baking sheet and place in the freezer for about 1 hour. Transfer the slices to gallon-size freezer bags. (Pre-freezing the toast on the baking sheet keeps the slices from sticking together.) To reheat, defrost the slices in the refrigerator overnight. Preheat the oven to 375°F. Place the French toast slices on a baking sheet sprayed with nonstick cooking spray and cover with aluminum foil. Heat in the oven for about 10 minutes and serve.

Per Serving: Calories: 272; Total fat: 10g; Sodium: 311mg; Carbohydrates: 36g; Fiber: 2g; Sugar: 12g; Protein: 10g

Apple-Cinnamon Oatmeal

SERVES 4 / PREP TIME: 5 MINUTES / COOK TIME: 10 MINUTES

Oatmeal is hearty and absorbs spices and other flavors really well. Plus, the apples and cinnamon fill the air with their delightful aromas. I love to drizzle a little maple syrup over the top of this recipe. What morning could be better?

1 teaspoon butter

1 large apple, peeled, cored, and chopped

½ teaspoon ground cinnamon

¼ teaspoon salt

1 cup old-fashioned oats

½ teaspoon pure maple syrup

OPTIONAL TOPPINGS:

Dried fruit and nuts, such as raisins, dried cranberries, almonds, and walnuts

1. In a 3-quart saucepan over medium heat, melt the butter. Add the apples and cook until soft, 2 to 3 minutes. Add the cinnamon, salt, and 2 cups of water, stir to combine, and bring to a boil.
2. Add the oats and maple syrup and stir to combine. Reduce the heat to medium-low and let simmer until the liquid is absorbed, 5 to 6 minutes.
3. Spoon into bowls, add any toppings (if using), and serve hot.

Addition Tips:
- Instead of apples, add 1 cup of blueberries, 1 cup of raspberries, 1 cup of strawberries, 1 chopped peach, or 1 chopped banana.
- Instead of water, add 2 cups of whole milk or almond milk for a creamier oatmeal.

Per Serving: Calories: 114; Total fat: 3g; Sodium: 146mg; Carbohydrates: 22g; Fiber: 3g; Sugar: 7g; Protein: 3g

Soups and Salads

< Mom's Homemade Tomato Soup, page 24

Mom's Homemade Tomato Soup

FREEZER-FRIENDLY / GLUTEN-FREE / NUT-FREE / ONE-POT

SERVES 4 / PREP TIME: 5 MINUTES / COOK TIME: 25 MINUTES

Rich and hearty, this tomato soup is a big bowl of comfort, and it's one of my family's favorites. Chock-full of tomatoes and herbs, this soup fills the air with irresistible smells that call you to the dinner table. Serve with the Go-To Chopped Salad (page 30), Classic Chicken Salad (page 34), or Easy Garlic Crostini (page 77), then kick back and enjoy.

1 teaspoon butter or olive oil

1 onion, chopped

2 garlic cloves, chopped

2 (14-ounce) cans diced tomatoes

2 cups vegetable or chicken stock

1 teaspoon Italian Herb Seasoning Mix (page 97)

OPTIONAL TOPPINGS:

Grated Parmigiano-Reggiano cheese

Chopped fresh basil or dried basil

1. In an 8-quart stockpot over medium heat, melt the butter. Add the onions and garlic and sauté until soft, about 3 minutes. Add the tomatoes, vegetable stock, and Italian herb seasoning. Stir to combine and bring to a boil.

2. Reduce the heat to medium-low. Using an immersion blender, purée the soup until smooth. Alternatively, carefully transfer the soup to a blender and purée until smooth. Simmer the soup until heated through, about 10 minutes. Taste and adjust the seasoning, if needed. Spoon into bowls, garnish with the Parmigiano-Reggiano cheese and basil (if using), and serve hot.

Storage Tip: Freeze for up to 3 months in a freezer-safe container. To reheat, defrost the soup overnight in the refrigerator. Reheat in a saucepan over low heat for 10 minutes until cooked through.

Cooking Tip: Be careful using any kind of blender with hot liquids. Hold the cover of the blender down with a kitchen towel while puréeing the hot soup. If using a closed-up blender, like a NutriBullet, let the soup cool slightly before puréeing. If using an immersion blender, be careful not to lift the blender, which could splash hot soup all over you and your kitchen.

Per Serving: Calories: 118; Total fat: 1g; Sodium: 1,243mg; Carbohydrates: 18g; Fiber: 4g; Sugar: 13g; Protein: 5g

VARIATIONS

Taco Tomato Soup
Add Beef Taco Filling (page 60) after puréeing the soup. Stir to combine and simmer for 10 minutes. Taste and adjust the seasoning, if needed.
Per Serving: Calories: 466; Total fat: 26g; Sodium: 2,037mg; Carbohydrates: 27g; Fiber: 6g; Sugar: 16g; Protein: 26g

Creamy Tomato Soup
After puréeing the soup and letting it simmer for 5 minutes, add ½ cup of heavy cream and stir to combine. Let simmer for an additional 5 minutes until heated through. Taste and adjust the seasoning, if needed, and serve.
Per Serving: Calories: 221; Total fat: 12g; Sodium: 1,254mg; Carbohydrates: 19g; Fiber: 4g; Sugar: 14g; Protein: 5g

Tortellini Tomato Soup
After puréeing the soup, add 8 ounces of fresh cheese tortellini and stir to combine. Let simmer for 10 minutes until cooked through. Taste and adjust the seasoning, if needed.
Per Serving: Calories: 231; Total fat: 6g; Sodium: 1,525mg; Carbohydrates: 29g; Fiber: 5g; Sugar: 14g; Protein: 10g

Basil Pesto Tomato Soup
After puréeing the soup, add 2 tablespoons of Nut-Free Basil Pesto (page 98) and stir to combine. Let simmer for 10 minutes until cooked through. Taste and adjust the seasoning, if needed.
Per Serving: Calories: 136; Total fat: 3g; Sodium: 1,258mg; Carbohydrates: 18g; Fiber: 4g; Sugar: 13g; Protein: 5g

Spinach Tomato Soup
After puréeing the soup, simmer for 5 minutes, then add 2 cups of chopped fresh spinach and stir to combine. Let simmer for an additional 5 minutes until cooked through. Taste and adjust the seasoning, if needed.
Per Serving: Calories: 124; Total fat: 1g; Sodium: 1,255mg; Carbohydrates: 19g; Fiber: 4g; Sugar: 13g; Protein: 5g

Taco Soup

FREEZER-FRIENDLY / GLUTEN-FREE / NUT-FREE / ONE-POT

SERVES 4 / PREP TIME: 10 MINUTES / COOK TIME: 20 MINUTES

This zesty soup hits the spot with the perfect amount of spice. For an easy shortcut, use the meat from the Beef Taco Filling (page 60) instead of the ground beef and the taco seasoning as the base for this recipe.

1 pound lean ground beef

1 (14-ounce) can spicy chili beans

4 cups beef broth

1 (15-ounce) jar mild salsa

1 teaspoon Taco Seasoning Mix (page 97)

OPTIONAL TOPPINGS:

Classic Guacamole (page 76)

Shredded Mexican-style cheese

Sour cream

1. In an 8-quart stockpot over medium-high heat, brown the ground beef, breaking it up with a spoon, until cooked through. Drain and discard any fat.

2. Add the chili beans, beef broth, salsa, and taco seasoning. Stir to combine. Bring to a boil, reduce the heat to medium-low, and let simmer for about 15 minutes. Taste and adjust the seasoning, if needed.

3. Spoon into bowls and top with guacamole, shredded cheese, and sour cream (if using).

Storage Tip: Freeze the soup in a freezer-safe container for up to 3 months. To reheat, defrost the soup overnight in the refrigerator. Reheat the soup in a saucepan over low heat for about 15 minutes, until heated through.

Substitution Tips:
- Use 1 pound of ground chicken or turkey instead of beef.
- For a gluten-free soup, check the label on the can of beans to be sure they are gluten-free.

Cooking Tips:
- Instead of using the Taco Seasoning Mix, use 1 teaspoon of cumin, ½ teaspoon of salt, and ½ teaspoon of freshly ground black pepper.
- Spicy chili beans are sold in the beans and Mexican foods section of most grocery stores. They are beans with added chili sauces and spices.

Per Serving: Calories: 458; Total fat: 25g; Sodium: 1,748mg; Carbohydrates: 27g; Fiber: 8g; Sugar: 5g; Protein: 32g

Shortcut Veggie Soup

SERVES 4 / PREP TIME: 5 MINUTES / COOK TIME: 20 MINUTES

Eat your vegetables with this wonderful soup that's loaded with nutrition. Frozen assorted vegetables speed up the process without sacrificing flavor. Keep frozen veggies in the freezer to make this soup anytime. Serve it with Go-To Chopped Salad (page 30), Classic Chicken Salad (page 34), or Easy Garlic Crostini (page 77) to complete the meal.

1 teaspoon olive oil

1 onion, diced

2 celery stalks, chopped

3 cups vegetable or chicken stock

1 tablespoon Italian Herb Seasoning Mix (page 97)

1 (16-ounce) bag frozen mixed peas, carrots, and beans

Salt

Freshly ground black pepper

1. In a stockpot over medium heat, warm the olive oil. Add the onions and celery and sauté until softened, about 3 minutes.

2. Add the vegetable stock and Italian herb seasoning and stir to combine. Increase the heat to medium-high and bring the soup to a boil. Reduce the heat to medium-low, add the frozen vegetables, and stir to combine. Let simmer for 10 to 15 minutes until the vegetables are fork-tender and heated through. Taste and adjust the seasoning with salt and pepper, if needed.

Storage Tip: Freeze the soup for up to 3 months. To reheat, defrost the soup overnight in the refrigerator. Reheat in a saucepan over low heat for about 10 minutes until heated through.

Substitution Tip: Use a frozen vegetable blend of broccoli, cauliflower, and carrots instead of peas, carrots, and beans.

Cooking Tip: If you don't have Italian Herb Seasoning Mix made, use ½ teaspoon of freshly ground black pepper, ½ teaspoon of salt, and 1 teaspoon of Italian seasoning.

Addition Tip: For a heartier soup, add 8 ounces of sliced mushrooms when you add the onions and celery.

Per Serving: Calories: 120; Total fat: 1g; Sodium: 1,084mg; Carbohydrates: 20g; Fiber: 3g; Sugar: 8g; Protein: 5g

Tuscan Bean Soup

SERVES 4 / PREP TIME: 5 MINUTES / COOK TIME: 20 MINUTES

Delicious and easy to make, this soup will warm your toes on a cold day. The flavors of white beans and spinach go together well and are quite flavorful. Add some grated Parmigiano-Reggiano to top off this delectable soup or pair it with a Go-To Chopped Salad (page 30), Classic Chicken Salad (page 34), or slices of warm crusty bread.

1 tablespoon olive oil

1 onion, diced

8 ounces turkey or chicken sausage, casing removed

4 cups chicken stock

½ teaspoon salt

½ teaspoon pepper

1 (15-ounce) can cannellini beans, drained and rinsed

8 ounces fresh spinach

OPTIONAL TOPPING:

Grated Parmigiano-Reggiano cheese

1. In a large stockpot over medium heat, warm the olive oil. Add the onions and sausage and sauté, breaking up the sausage with a spoon, until the meat is no longer pink, 3 to 4 minutes.

2. Add the chicken stock, salt, and pepper. Stir to combine. Increase the heat to medium-high and bring the soup to a boil. Add the beans and spinach, reduce the heat to medium-low, and simmer until cooked through, 4 to 5 minutes. Taste and adjust the seasoning with salt and pepper, if needed. Top with Parmigiano-Reggiano cheese (if using) and serve.

Storage Tip: Freeze the soup in a freezer-safe container for up to 3 months. To reheat, defrost the soup overnight in the refrigerator. Reheat in a saucepan over low heat for about 10 minutes until heated through.

Substitution Tip: For a vegetarian soup, do not add the sausage. Instead, add 1 (14-ounce) can of diced tomatoes with the stock, substituting the chicken stock for vegetable stock.

Cooking Tip: For a boost of flavor, instead of salt and pepper, add 1 teaspoon of Italian Herb Seasoning Mix (page 97).

Per Serving: Calories: 274; Total fat: 11g; Sodium: 1,338mg; Carbohydrates: 27g; Fiber: 7g; Sugar: 6g; Protein: 19g

Feel Better Chicken Noodle Soup

SERVES 4 / PREP TIME: 10 MINUTES / COOK TIME: 20 MINUTES

This is a spin on one of my most popular recipes. As you get comfortable making this soup, expand to add your favorite seasonings. For a low-carb version, use 6 ounces of uncooked zoodles (page 82) instead of egg noodles.

1 tablespoon olive oil

2 celery stalks, peeled and chopped

2 carrots, peeled and chopped

1 pound chicken tenderloins, cut into 1-inch pieces

½ teaspoon salt

½ teaspoon freshly ground black pepper

4 cups chicken stock

6 ounces fine egg noodles

1. In a stockpot over medium heat, warm the olive oil. Add the celery, carrots, and chicken. Sauté until the vegetables are softened and the chicken is cooked, about 5 minutes. Add the salt and pepper and stir to combine.

2. Add the chicken stock, increase the heat to medium-high, and bring to a boil. Reduce the heat and simmer for 5 minutes. Add the fine egg noodles and simmer until the noodles are tender, another 5 minutes. Taste and adjust the seasoning with salt and pepper, if needed.

Storage Tip: This soup freezes very well in a freezer-safe container for up to 3 months. To reheat, defrost in the refrigerator overnight. Reheat in a saucepan over medium-low heat for about 10 minutes until heated through. The noodles may soak up some of the chicken stock. If needed, add 1 cup of chicken broth to the saucepan when reheating.

Per Serving: Calories: 314; Total fat: 6g; Sodium: 891mg; Carbohydrates: 34g; Fiber: 3g; Sugar: 3g; Protein: 31g

Go-To Chopped Salad

SERVES 4 / PREP TIME: 10 MINUTES

Everyone needs an easy and delicious house salad that they can throw together at a moment's notice. Topped with a homemade vinaigrette that complements the fresh greens and veggies, this salad is simplicity at its best. It will keep well in the refrigerator for a few days.

4 cups chopped salad greens

1 pint grape tomatoes, cut in half

1 large cucumber, peeled and diced

1 large carrot, peeled and chopped

¼ cup House Salad Dressing (page 99)

1. In a large bowl, mix the salad greens, grape tomatoes, cucumber, and carrots.
2. Toss with the dressing and serve.

Per Serving: Calories: 138; Total fat: 9g; Sodium: 131mg; Carbohydrates: 12g; Fiber: 3g; Sugar: 6g; Protein: 3g

VARIATIONS

Bacon Chopped Salad

Replace the carrots with 8 ounces of cooked, crumbled bacon.

Per Serving: Calories: 221; Total fat: 16g; Sodium: 359mg; Carbohydrates: 11g; Fiber: 3g; Sugar: 5g; Protein: 8g

Chicken Chopped Salad

Replace the carrots with 8 ounces of sliced Easy Baked Chicken Breasts (page 48).

Per Serving: Calories: 204; Total fat: 11g; Sodium: 224mg; Carbohydrates: 11g; Fiber: 3g; Sugar: 5g; Protein: 14g

Chickpea Chopped Salad

Replace the carrots with 1 (14-ounce) can of drained and rinsed chickpeas.

Per Serving: Calories: 236; Total fat: 10g; Sodium: 119mg; Carbohydrates: 30g; Fiber: 8g; Sugar: 5g; Protein: 8g

Tuna Chopped Salad

Replace the carrots with 2 (5-ounce) cans of drained tuna.

Per Serving: Calories: 176; Total fat: 10g; Sodium: 299mg; Carbohydrates: 11g; Fiber: 3g; Sugar: 5g; Protein: 13g

Fruit and Nut Chopped Salad

Replace the cucumbers and carrots with 4 ounces of dried fruit (cranberries or apricots, for example) and 3 ounces of nuts (pecans or walnuts, for example).

Per Serving: Calories: 313; Total fat: 19g; Sodium: 121mg; Carbohydrates: 33g; Fiber: 4g; Sugar: 6g; Protein: 5g

Creamy Macaroni and Broccoli Salad

SERVES 4 / PREP TIME: 10 MINUTES / COOK TIME: 12 MINUTES

A great macaroni salad is a must-have recipe to keep in your back pocket. It's versatile and a great side for Build Your Burger (page 62), Easy Baked Chicken Breasts (page 48), or Pan-Seared Pork Chops and Parmesan Spinach (page 66). This recipe sneaks in some veggies for a protein-packed salad that is hearty enough to be a light lunch or meatless dinner.

8 ounces macaroni or small pasta shells

2 cups bite-size broccoli florets

1 cup Homemade Dijonnaise (page 100) or 1 cup mayonnaise

4 ounces grape tomatoes, chopped

1 cup shredded Cheddar cheese

Salt

Freshly ground black pepper

1. Bring a large stockpot of water to a boil and cook the pasta according to the package instructions.
2. Three minutes before the pasta is cooked, add the broccoli. Drain and set aside in a large bowl.
3. Add the Dijonnaise, grape tomatoes, and Cheddar cheese. Mix to combine. Taste and adjust the seasoning with salt and pepper.

Substitution Tips:
- Instead of the Cheddar cheese, add 1 (5-ounce) can of drained tuna.
- Instead of the broccoli, use 2 cups of cauliflower florets.

Cooking Tip: This is a great make-ahead salad because it can keep in the refrigerator for up to 4 days.

Per Serving: Calories: 1,039; Total fat: 83g; Sodium: 1,132mg; Carbohydrates: 46g; Fiber: 3g; Sugar: 12g; Protein: 20g

Lemony Lentil Salad

SERVES 4 / PREP TIME: 10 MINUTES / COOK TIME: 20 MINUTES

Preparing lentils is easier than you think, and they are full of amazing flavor. This healthy lentil salad recipe is ready in no time and is a perfect make-ahead salad. Enjoy it all week, as it can be kept in the refrigerator for up to 5 days. Try the salad with Easy Baked Chicken Breasts (page 48), Pan-Seared Pork Chops and Parmesan Spinach (page 66), or Build Your Burger (page 62).

1 cup red lentils, rinsed

¼ teaspoon salt

1 shallot, diced

½ cup chopped carrots

⅓ cup chopped celery

Lemony House Dressing (page 99)

1. In a saucepan over medium-high heat, mix the lentils and 4 cups of water.
2. Bring to a boil. Reduce the heat to low and simmer for 15 minutes. Drain the lentils and mix in the salt.
3. In a medium bowl, mix the lentils, shallot, carrots, and celery. Toss with the Lemony House Dressing.

Substitution Tips:
- If you do not have Lemony House Dressing on hand, use a store-bought dressing that you love.
- Brown lentils can be used instead of red, but they can take as long as 25 minutes to cook. Check the package for cooking times.
- Swap out any of the vegetables for ¼ cup of sun-dried tomatoes or 4 ounces of chopped tomatoes.

Per Serving: Calories: 439; Total fat: 37g; Sodium: 486mg; Carbohydrates: 29g; Fiber: 9g; Sugar: 2g; Protein: 10g

Classic Chicken Salad

SERVES 4 / PREP TIME: 10 MINUTES / COOK TIME: 15 MINUTES

I think chicken salad is pure comfort food, and it's an absolute treat to eat. With just a few simple, delicious ingredients, this salad works for lunch or as a light dinner served with a bowl of soup. Put it between two slices of bread and it makes a great sandwich, too. The Homemade Dijonnaise (page 100) is the secret sauce that makes this recipe so tasty.

1½ pounds boneless, skinless chicken breasts, cut into 1-inch pieces

1 stalk celery, finely chopped

1 large carrot, peeled and diced

1 green onion, finely chopped

½ cup Homemade Dijonnaise (page 100) or ½ cup mayonnaise

Salt

Freshly ground black pepper

1. In a small saucepan over medium heat, add the chicken and enough water to cover the pieces completely.
2. Bring to a low boil and cook until the chicken is cooked through and no longer pink, about 10 minutes. Transfer the chicken to a plate and let cool slightly. Chop or shred the chicken.
3. In a medium bowl, mix the cooked chicken, celery, carrot, green onion, and Dijonnaise. Taste and adjust the seasoning with salt and pepper, if needed.

Storage Tip: Chicken salad will stay fresh in an airtight container in the refrigerator for up to 3 days.

Addition Tip: Add 4 ounces of dried cranberries or 4 ounces of green grapes with the chicken.

Cooking Tip: Use leftover chicken from Easy Baked Chicken Breasts (page 48) or use a store-bought rotisserie chicken.

Substitution Tip: For a gluten-free recipe, use mayonnaise instead of the Homemade Dijonnaise. If you want to use the Dijonnaise, be sure to make it with a gluten-free Worcestershire sauce.

Per Serving: Calories: 469; Total fat: 36g; Sodium: 671mg; Carbohydrates: 2g; Fiber: 1g; Sugar: 5g; Protein: 35g

Steakhouse Salad

SERVES 4 / PREP TIME: 10 MINUTES / COOK TIME: 10 MINUTES

No need to leave the house for a mouthwatering salad with juicy sliced steak and blue cheese crumbles over a crispy bed of greens. Inspiration for this recipe came from a favorite steakhouse that brought this delightful salad together quickly. Serve with Easy Garlic Crostini (page 77).

1 teaspoon olive oil

1 (12-ounce) sirloin steak

½ teaspoon salt

½ teaspoon freshly ground black pepper

4 cups chopped salad greens

½ cup grape tomatoes, cut in half

¾ cup blue cheese, crumbled

½ cup House Salad Dressing (page 99)

1. In a skillet over medium-high heat, warm the olive oil.

2. Season the steak with salt and pepper. Add the steak to the pan and cook to your desired level of doneness. For a rare steak, cook 3 minutes per side. For a medium steak, 4 minutes per side. For a medium-well steak, 5 minutes per side. Let the steak rest about 5 minutes before cutting into slices.

3. In a large bowl, arrange the salad greens, grape tomatoes, and blue cheese. Place the sliced steak on top of the greens and serve with the dressing.

Addition Tip: Add ½ cup of sliced carrots, 1 diced shallot, and ½ cup of croutons to the salad greens, grape tomatoes, and blue cheese.

Substitution Tip: Instead of salt and pepper, use ½ teaspoon of Seasoned Salt (page 96).

Per Serving: Calories: 495; Total fat: 36g; Sodium: 1,138mg; Carbohydrates: 6g; Fiber: 1g; Sugar: 1g; Protein: 36g

Vegan and Vegetarian Mains

< Spinach and Mushroom Frittata, page 42

Cheesy Pesto Flatbread

SERVES 4 / PREP TIME: 5 MINUTES / COOK TIME: 10 MINUTES

You will never want takeout again after making these tasty flatbreads. Made with Nut-Free Basil Pesto (page 98), peppery arugula, sun-dried tomatoes, and cheese, it's substantial enough to make a satisfying dinner. You can find flatbread in the bread aisle of your grocery store.

Nonstick cooking spray

4 flatbreads

1 cup Nut-Free Basil Pesto (page 98)

1 cup shredded mozzarella cheese

⅓ cup diced sun-dried tomatoes

1½ cups arugula

2 teaspoons olive oil

½ teaspoon freshly ground black pepper

¼ teaspoon salt

1. Preheat the oven to 400°F. Spray a baking sheet with nonstick cooking spray.
2. Lay out the flatbreads on the prepared baking sheet. Spread the pesto equally over the flatbreads. Sprinkle the mozzarella over the pesto and scatter the sun-dried tomatoes equally.
3. Bake for 10 minutes, until the cheese is melted.
4. While the flatbreads are in the oven, place the arugula in a bowl and drizzle the olive oil over it. Season with the salt and pepper.
5. Distribute the arugula over the flatbreads and serve.

Per Serving: Calories: 412; Total fat: 25g; Sodium: 1,173mg; Carbohydrates: 22g; Fiber: 9g; Sugar: 2g; Protein: 25g

VARIATIONS

Sweet Pepper, Onion, and Fontina Cheese Flatbread Pizza

Drizzle 2 tablespoons of olive oil in a medium skillet over medium heat. Add 2 thinly sliced red and yellow bell peppers, and 1 thinly sliced onion. Sauté until softened, about 5 minutes. Set aside. Spread 1 cup of marinara equally over 4 flatbreads. Sprinkle with ⅓ cup of shredded fontina cheese and top with the peppers and onions. Season with salt and pepper. Bake on a baking sheet sprayed with nonstick cooking spray in a 400°F oven for 10 minutes until the cheese is melted.

Per Serving: Calories: 277; Total fat: 12g; Sodium: 600mg; Carbohydrates: 29g; Fiber: 11g; Sugar: 6g; Protein: 15g

Broccoli, Mushroom, and Cheddar Flatbread Pizza

Spread 4 flatbreads equally with 1 cup of Nut-Free Basil Pesto (page 98) and place them on a baking sheet sprayed with nonstick cooking spray. Sprinkle 1 cup of shredded Cheddar cheese, 1 cup of broccoli florets, and ½ cup of chopped mushrooms equally over the flatbreads. Season with salt and pepper. Bake in a 400°F oven for 10 minutes, or until the cheese is melted.

Per Serving: Calories: 417; Total fat: 27g; Sodium: 947mg; Carbohydrates: 20g; Fiber: 9g; Sugar: 1g; Protein: 23g

Smoky Chickpeas and Spinach

SERVES 4 / PREP TIME: 5 MINUTES / COOK TIME: 8 MINUTES

The Mediterranean flavors are flowing in this popular Spanish recipe known as *espinacas con garbanzos*. The smoked paprika is what really makes this dish distinctive, so don't substitute it with plain paprika.

2 tablespoons olive oil

1 small onion, diced

3 garlic cloves, minced

12 ounces fresh baby spinach or defrosted frozen spinach

1 teaspoon smoked paprika

2 (14-ounce) cans chickpeas, drained and rinsed

¼ teaspoon salt

½ teaspoon freshly ground black pepper

1. In a large skillet over medium heat, warm the olive oil. Add the onion and cook until softened, about 4 minutes. Add the garlic and cook until fragrant, about 1 minute. Add the spinach and smoked paprika, stir to combine, and cook until wilted.

2. Add the chickpeas, salt, and pepper. Stir to combine. Simmer until the chickpeas are heated through, about 2 minutes. Taste and adjust the seasoning with salt and pepper, if needed.

Substitution Tip: Instead of spinach, substitute 12 ounces of escarole or kale, and use another favorite bean instead of chickpeas.

Per Serving: Calories: 302; Total fat: 9g; Sodium: 212mg; Carbohydrates: 44g; Fiber: 13g; Sugar: 1g; Protein: 13g

Coconut Tofu and Vegetable Curry over Rice

SERVES 4 / PREP TIME: 5 MINUTES / COOK TIME: 20 MINUTES

One of my favorite time-savers is to use frozen veggies in recipes like this so I don't need to spend a lot of time cutting up fresh vegetables. Serve this on a chilly weeknight, and your family will thank you.

1 (13.5-ounce) can coconut milk, divided

1 cup basmati rice, rinsed

6 ounces firm tofu, patted dry

2 teaspoons olive oil

12 ounces frozen broccoli, cauliflower, and carrot blend

1 tablespoon yellow curry paste

Salt

1. In a medium saucepan over medium heat, mix 1 cup of the coconut milk, rice, and ¾ cup of water. Increase the heat to high, bring to a boil, and cook, stirring, for 2 minutes. Reduce the heat to low. Cover the pan with a lid and let simmer, stirring occasionally, until the rice is cooked, about 15 minutes. Remove from the heat.

2. While the rice is cooking, press the tofu between layers of paper towels to release as much liquid as possible. Cut the tofu into 1-inch cubes.

3. In a skillet over medium heat, warm the olive oil. Add the tofu and brown on all sides, about 10 minutes.

4. Add the vegetables and cook, stirring, for 1 to 2 minutes. Reduce the heat to low, add the remaining coconut milk, yellow curry paste, and salt. Stir to combine. Let simmer until cooked through, about 8 minutes. Taste and adjust the seasoning with more curry paste or salt, if needed.

5. Spoon the rice into bowls and pour the tofu and vegetables over the top.

Substitution Tip: Instead of tofu, add 8 ounces of cooked chickpeas with the vegetables and cook as instructed.

Per Serving: Calories: 461; Total fat: 22g; Sodium: 270mg; Carbohydrates: 54g; Fiber: 5g; Sugar: 2g; Protein: 12g

Spinach and Mushroom Frittata

SERVES 4 / PREP TIME: 5 MINUTES / COOK TIME: 20 MINUTES

Frittatas are such an easy dinner to prepare, and the leftovers are great for lunch the next day, especially paired with the Go-To Chopped Salad (page 30) or the Easy Garlic Crostini (page 77). This is also a great recipe to use as a base to use up leftovers in the refrigerator. Have some leftover bacon or turkey? A few vegetables? Add it to your frittata. Use an oven-safe pan, such as a cast iron skillet, as this recipe begins on the stovetop and finishes in the oven.

6 eggs

¼ cup milk

½ teaspoon freshly ground black pepper

½ teaspoon salt

1 teaspoon olive oil

1 cup diced mushrooms

2 cups fresh spinach

1 cup shredded fontina cheese

1. Preheat the oven to 400°F.

2. In a medium bowl, whisk together the eggs, milk, pepper, and salt. Set aside.

3. In a large oven-safe skillet over medium heat, warm the olive oil. Add the mushrooms and sauté until soft, about 3 minutes. Add the spinach and cook until wilted. Sprinkle the shredded cheese into the skillet.

4. Pour the egg mixture into the skillet and let cook undisturbed for 5 minutes.

5. Place the skillet into the oven and bake until the eggs are set, 10 to 12 minutes. Let cool for 2 minutes before slicing and serving.

Substitution Tip: Use Gruyère, Cheddar, Swiss, or mozzarella instead of fontina.

Addition Tip: Add 1 teaspoon of Italian Herb Seasoning Mix (page 97) to the egg mixture. For meat lovers, add 4 ounces of diced ham along with the mushrooms.

Per Serving: Calories: 212; Total fat: 15g; Sodium: 577mg; Carbohydrates: 3g; Fiber: 1g; Sugar: 1g; Protein: 15g

Mexican Stuffed Peppers

SERVES 4 / PREP TIME: 10 MINUTES / COOK TIME: 15 MINUTES

You will just love the kick of flavor from these Mexican-inspired stuffed peppers. These tasty treats are perfect on their own or alongside Taco Soup (page 26) or Sheet Pan Nachos (page 78).

Nonstick cooking spray

4 bell peppers, seeded and cut in half lengthwise

1 cup refried beans

1 (16-ounce) can spicy chili beans

4 ounces whipped cream cheese

½ teaspoon salt

½ teaspoon freshly ground black pepper

1 cup shredded Mexican-style cheese

1. Preheat the oven to 400°F. Spray a 9-by-13-inch baking pan with nonstick cooking spray.
2. Place the peppers skin-side down in the prepared baking pan.
3. In a medium bowl, mix the refried beans, chili beans, whipped cream cheese, salt, and pepper.
4. Spoon the refried bean mixture equally among the peppers. Sprinkle the peppers with the shredded cheese.
5. Cover the pan with aluminum foil and bake for 15 minutes. If the cheese is not fully melted, place the pan under the broiler for 5 to 10 seconds to melt the cheese.
6. Serve hot.

Storage Tip: The stuffed peppers can be frozen in a resealable, freezer-safe bag for up to 3 months. To reheat, defrost in the refrigerator overnight. Place the peppers on a baking sheet and heat in a 350°F oven for 15 minutes. You can cook them directly from the freezer by placing them in a baking dish, covering the pan with aluminum foil, and baking for about 30 minutes.

Substitution Tip: Use 1 teaspoon of Taco Seasoning Mix (page 97) instead of salt and pepper.

Per Serving: Calories: 327; Total fat: 11g; Sodium: 1,223mg; Carbohydrates: 38g; Fiber: 12g; Sugar: 5g; Protein: 19g

Pasta Primavera in a Creamy Tomato Sauce

SERVES 4 / PREP TIME: 10 MINUTES / COOK TIME: 20 MINUTES

You are going to love this wonderful one-pot meal. The vegetables are cooked in the pot with the pasta, so dinner can be on the table in a flash. Pair this with the Easy Garlic Crostini (page 77) or the Go-To Chopped Salad (page 30).

1½ cups vegetable stock

½ teaspoon salt, plus more if needed

8 ounces spaghetti

1 cup frozen vegetable mix such as Normandy blend, if available

1 cup marinara sauce

3 ounces cream cheese

½ teaspoon freshly ground black pepper

OPTIONAL GARNISH:

Grated Parmesan cheese

1. In a large stockpot over medium-high heat, mix the vegetable stock, 1½ cups of water, salt, and spaghetti. Bring to a boil, stirring occasionally.
2. Reduce the heat to medium, add the frozen vegetables. Let simmer, stirring occasionally, until the pasta is cooked and the liquid is mostly absorbed, about 10 minutes.
3. Add the marinara sauce, cream cheese, and pepper. Stir to combine. Cook for about 2 minutes, or until cooked through. Taste and adjust the seasoning with salt and pepper, if needed. Serve warm.

Substitution Tip: Instead of salt and pepper, add 1 teaspoon of Italian Herb Seasoning Mix (page 97) to the stockpot with the vegetable stock and water.

Cooking Tip: Normandy blend is mix of broccoli, carrots, cauliflower, yellow squash, and zucchini. Any blend of frozen vegetables will work in this recipe. Choose the one you like best.

Per Serving: Calories: 323; Total fat: 10g; Sodium: 824mg; Carbohydrates: 49g; Fiber: 3g; Sugar: 7g; Protein: 11g

Poultry and Seafood

< Balsamic-and-Honey-Glazed Salmon, page 57

Easy Baked Chicken Breasts

DAIRY-FREE / FREEZER-FRIENDLY / GLUTEN-FREE / NUT-FREE / SHEET PAN

SERVES 4 / PREP TIME: 5 MINUTES / COOK TIME: 15 TO 20 MINUTES

This chicken is tender and juicy with the most aromatic seasoning. Different seasonings can be used on the chicken to change up the flavors, producing delicious results every time. Try herbs like rosemary, thyme, and parsley. Try Nut-Free Basil Pesto (page 98) or chopped sun-dried tomatoes. Rubbing the chicken with ground cumin and paprika will add bold and zesty flavors. Pair with Garlic-Roasted Potatoes (page 80), Garlic Butter Rice (page 81), or Roasted Lemon Asparagus (page 85).

Nonstick cooking spray

1 teaspoon olive oil

4 boneless, skinless chicken breasts, about 1½ inches thick

1½ teaspoons Seasoned Salt (page 96)

OPTIONAL GARNISH:

Chopped fresh parsley

1. Preheat the oven to 425°F. Spray a baking pan with nonstick cooking spray. Set aside.
2. Rub the olive oil on both sides of the chicken breasts. Sprinkle the seasoned salt on the chicken breasts, being sure to coat both sides.
3. Place the chicken breasts into the baking pan and bake for 15 minutes, until the chicken reaches an internal temperature of 165°F. Garnish with fresh parsley (if using).

Storage Tip: Cooked chicken breasts can be kept in an airtight container in the refrigerator for 2 days. To freeze, place the cooked chicken on a baking sheet and freeze for about 1 hour. Transfer the chicken to a freezer-safe container or freezer bags and freeze for up to 3 months. To reheat, defrost the chicken overnight in the refrigerator. Place the chicken on a baking sheet, cover with aluminum foil, and bake in a 325°F oven for about 10 minutes until heated through.

Per Serving: Calories: 123; Total fat: 4g; Sodium: 475mg; Carbohydrates: 1g; Fiber: 0g; Sugar: 0g; Protein: 23g

VARIATIONS

Mexican Chicken Breasts

Preheat the oven to 425°F. Rub 4 boneless, skinless chicken breasts with 1 teaspoon of olive oil and 1 teaspoon of lime juice. Sprinkle 1½ teaspoons of Taco Seasoning Mix (page 97) on the chicken breasts, making sure to coat both sides. Bake as instructed and garnish with chopped fresh cilantro.

Per Serving: Calories: 123; Total fat: 4g; Sodium: 475mg; Carbohydrates: 1g; Fiber: 0g; Sugar: 0g; Protein: 23g

Italian Herb Chicken Breasts

Preheat the oven to 425°F. Rub 4 boneless, skinless chicken breasts with 1 teaspoon of olive oil and 1 teaspoon of lemon juice. Sprinkle 1½ teaspoons of Italian Herb Seasoning Mix (page 97) and ½ teaspoon of red pepper flakes, if you like spicy food, on the chicken breasts, making sure to coat both sides. Bake as instructed and garnish with chopped fresh basil.

Per Serving: Calories: 123; Total fat: 4g; Sodium: 475mg; Carbohydrates: 1g; Fiber: 0g; Sugar: 0g; Protein: 23g

Cajun Chicken Breasts

Preheat the oven to 425°F. Rub 4 boneless, skinless chicken breasts with 1 teaspoon of olive oil and 1 teaspoon of lime juice. Sprinkle 1½ teaspoons of Cajun Seasoning Mix (page 97) on the chicken breasts, making sure to coat both sides. Bake as instructed and garnish with chopped fresh parsley.

Per Serving: Calories: 123; Total fat: 4g; Sodium: 475mg; Carbohydrates: 1g; Fiber: 0g; Sugar: 0g; Protein: 23g

Baked Parmesan Chicken Tenders

SERVES 4 / PREP TIME: 10 MINUTES / COOK TIME: 15 MINUTES

Chicken fingers are not just for kids. These crisp and juicy tenders are super easy and are perfect for dipping into Homemade Dijonnaise (page 100). Make a batch of Garlic-Roasted Potatoes (page 80) to serve alongside, and you'll enjoy a great dinner without spending money on takeout.

Nonstick cooking spray

2 eggs

¾ cup Italian bread crumbs

¼ cup grated Parmesan cheese

¾ teaspoon salt

¾ teaspoon freshly ground black pepper

1 pound chicken tenderloins

Homemade Dijonnaise (page 100), ketchup, or ranch dressing, for dipping

1. Preheat the oven to 400°F. Spray a baking sheet with nonstick cooking spray. Set aside.
2. In a medium shallow bowl, whisk the eggs and add a splash of water.
3. In a separate shallow bowl, combine the Italian bread crumbs, Parmesan cheese, salt, and pepper.
4. Dredge the chicken tenderloins in the egg mixture and then in the bread crumb mixture.
5. Place the breaded tenderloins onto the prepared baking sheet, ensuring they do not overlap for even cooking.
6. Bake for 8 minutes, turn the tenderloins over, and bake for an additional 7 minutes, until cooked through and crunchy.
7. Serve with the Dijonnaise on the side.

Storage Tip: Cooked chicken tenders can be kept in an airtight container in the refrigerator for 3 days. To freeze, place the cooked chicken on a baking sheet and freeze for about 1 hour. Transfer the chicken to a freezer-safe container or freezer bags and freeze for up to 3 months. To reheat, defrost the chicken overnight in the refrigerator. Place the chicken on a baking sheet, cover with aluminum foil, and bake in a 325°F oven for about 10 minutes until heated through.

Substitution Tip: Instead of salt and pepper, use 1½ teaspoons of Seasoned Salt (page 96).

Per Serving: Calories: 248; Total fat: 6g; Sodium: 1,051mg; Carbohydrates: 16g; Fiber: 1g; Sugar: 2g; Protein: 31g

Chicken, Asparagus, and Tomato Pesto Pasta

SERVES 4 / PREP TIME: 5 MINUTES / COOK TIME: 15 MINUTES

Enjoy a pesto-enhanced dinner of juicy chicken and fresh tomatoes over penne pasta. After a long day of work, you'll appreciate how quickly this recipe comes together, and it tastes great. Enjoy with some Easy Garlic Crostini (page 77).

12 ounces penne pasta

1 teaspoon olive oil

1 pound chicken tenderloins

Salt

Freshly ground black pepper

1 pound fresh asparagus, trimmed and cut into 1-inch pieces

8 ounces tomatoes, diced

1 cup Nut-Free Basil Pesto (page 98)

OPTIONAL GARNISHES:

Grated Parmesan cheese

Chopped fresh basil

1. Bring a large stockpot of water to a boil and cook the pasta according to the package instructions. Drain and set aside.

2. While the pasta cooks, in a sauté pan over medium heat, warm the olive oil. Season the chicken with salt and pepper and cook, stirring frequently, until the chicken browns, about 3 minutes. Add the asparagus and continue to sauté until the chicken and asparagus are cooked, about 8 minutes.

3. Add the diced tomatoes and basil pesto and cook, stirring occasionally, until heated through. Add the cooked pasta and stir to combine. Taste and adjust the seasoning with salt and pepper, if needed.

4. Serve with Parmesan cheese and chopped basil (if using).

Storage Tip: This can be stored in an airtight container in the refrigerator for up to 2 days.

Per Serving: Calories: 626; Total fat: 22g; Sodium: 659mg; Carbohydrates: 71g; Fiber: 6g; Sugar: 5g; Protein: 41g

Turkey Lettuce Wraps

DAIRY-FREE / FREEZER-FRIENDLY / NUT-FREE / ONE-PAN

SERVES 4 / PREP TIME: 5 MINUTES / COOK TIME: 15 MINUTES

The sweet and savory flavor of the Brown Sugar–Soy Sauce (page 101) is a classic combination that is absolutely delicious in these fun lettuce wraps. The lean turkey and vegetables also make this a healthy, balanced meal. You can't go wrong with that.

1 teaspoon olive oil

1 small onion, diced

1 large carrot, peeled and diced

1 pound lean ground turkey

½ cup Brown Sugar–Soy Sauce (page 101)

Salt

Freshly ground black pepper

4 large Bibb lettuce leaves

OPTIONAL GARNISH:

Chopped green onion

1. In a large skillet over medium heat, warm the olive oil. Add the onion and carrot and sauté until just softened, about 3 minutes. Add the ground turkey and cook, breaking up the meat with a spoon, until cooked through, about 8 minutes.

2. Add the brown sugar–soy sauce and simmer until heated through, 3 to 5 minutes. Taste and add salt and pepper, if needed.

3. Spoon the mixture into the lettuce and top with chopped green onion (if using).

Storage Tip: The cooked turkey mixture can be kept in an airtight container in the refrigerator for up to 2 days. To freeze, place the turkey mixture in a freezer-safe container or freezer bags and freeze for up to 2 months. To reheat, defrost overnight in the refrigerator. Reheat the turkey in a skillet over medium heat for about 5 minutes until heated through.

Per Serving: Calories: 201; Total fat: 9g; Sodium: 396mg; Carbohydrates: 7g; Fiber: 1g; Sugar: 4g; Protein: 23g

Sheet Pan Cajun Turkey Sausage with Potatoes and Peppers

SERVES 4 / PREP TIME: 10 MINUTES / COOK TIME: 20 MINUTES

Sheet pan dinners are such a time saver. Enjoy the Cajun flavors of this mouthwatering meal with smoked turkey sausage and baby potatoes roasted with green peppers. Bell peppers come in many different colors, so feel free to choose your favorite.

12 ounces cooked smoked turkey sausage, cut into 1-inch pieces

1 pound baby red or yellow potatoes, cut into ½-inch-thick slices

1 large bell pepper in any color, seeded and cut into 1-inch pieces

2 tablespoons olive oil

1 teaspoon Cajun Seasoning Mix (page 97)

1. Preheat the oven to 425°F. Have a baking sheet ready.
2. Place the turkey sausage, baby potatoes, and bell peppers on the baking sheet. Drizzle with the olive oil, sprinkle with the Cajun seasoning, and toss to combine.
3. Bake for 10 minutes. Flip the vegetables over and bake another 10 minutes. Serve immediately.

Storage Tip: This dish can be stored in an airtight container in the refrigerator for up to 2 days. This recipe does not freeze well.

Per Serving: Calories: 316; Total fat: 18g; Sodium: 1,041mg; Carbohydrates: 27g; Fiber: 4g; Sugar: 8g; Protein: 14g

Southern Shrimp and Grits

SERVES 4 / PREP TIME: 5 MINUTES / COOK TIME: 12 MINUTES

Spicy shrimp and bacon adorn bowls of creamy grits, making a savory and oh-so-satisfying Southern meal. This dish is best served immediately, though the shrimp can be kept in the refrigerator overnight.

1 cup quick-cooking grits

4 slices bacon, diced

1 onion, diced

1 pound shrimp, peeled and deveined

1 teaspoon Cajun Seasoning Mix (page 97)

Salt

Freshly ground black pepper

OPTIONAL GARNISHES:

Shredded Monterey Jack cheese

Chopped fresh parsley

1. In a medium saucepan, cook the grits according to the package instructions, about 7 minutes.

2. While the grits cook, in a sauté pan over medium heat, cook the bacon until crispy, about 5 minutes. Place the bacon on a paper towel-lined plate and set aside. Leave the bacon drippings in the pan.

3. Add the diced onion to the sauté pan and sauté over medium heat for about 3 minutes.

4. Toss the shrimp with the Cajun seasoning, add to the pan, and sauté until cooked through, about 2 minutes per side.

5. To serve, spoon the grits into a bowl and season with salt and pepper to taste. Top with diced bacon, shrimp, cheese, and parsley (if using).

Per Serving: Calories: 323; Total fat: 6g; Sodium: 562mg; Carbohydrates: 35g; Fiber: 1g; Sugar: 1g; Protein: 30g

Seared Sea Scallops

SERVES 4 / PREP TIME: 5 MINUTES / COOK TIME: 4 MINUTES

No need to go to an expensive seafood restaurant when you can make your own delicious scallop dinner at home. These scallops boast a crispy outside and a tender and juicy inside and are served with a decadent butter sauce. Serve with your favorite pasta or Garlic-Roasted Potatoes (page 80) on the side.

1 pound sea scallops

½ teaspoon salt

½ teaspoon freshly ground black pepper

2 tablespoons olive oil

4 tablespoons butter

Chopped fresh parsley, for garnish

Lemon wedges, for garnish

1. Pat the scallops dry with a paper towel to ensure they will sear properly. Season the scallops with the salt and pepper.

2. Preheat a large sauté pan over medium heat. Add the olive oil to the pan. Be sure to use a large enough pan so that the scallops are not crowded, or they will steam instead of searing and won't get crispy on the outside.

3. When the pan is very hot, add the scallops and let sear without disturbing them for about 2 minutes. Turn the scallops over and add the butter to the pan. Using a spoon, baste the scallops with the melted butter for about 1 minute.

4. Serve the scallops garnished with chopped parsley and lemon wedges on the side.

Storage Tip: The scallops are best eaten right away, but if necessary, you can store them in an airtight container in the refrigerator for 1 day. Reheat in a sauté pan over medium heat for about 2 to 3 minutes until just heated through.

Substitution Tip: Use 1 teaspoon of any of the seasonings in chapter 9 in place of the salt and pepper for seasoning the scallops. Continue to follow the recipe instructions.

Per Serving: Calories: 262; Total fat: 19g; Sodium: 475mg; Carbohydrates: 3g; Fiber: 0g; Sugar: 0g; Protein: 19g

Foil Packet Fish Fillets and Tomatoes

SERVES 4 / PREP TIME: 10 MINUTES / COOK TIME: 12 TO 15 MINUTES

This is an elegant yet easy meal that can be served for a quick weeknight dinner. It's also perfect for a special night with friends. Use a hearty fish like flounder, halibut, or salmon.

4 (6-ounce) flounder fillets

1 zucchini, cut into ½-inch slices

2 plum tomatoes, diced

4 teaspoons lemon juice

¼ teaspoon salt

¼ teaspoon freshly ground black pepper

Chopped fresh basil, for garnish

1. Preheat the oven to 425°F. Lay 4 sheets of aluminum foil on a large baking sheet.
2. Place 1 piece of flounder in the center of each sheet of foil. Distribute the zucchini and tomatoes equally over the fish.
3. Drizzle lemon juice over the fish and vegetables and season with salt and pepper.
4. Fold up two sides of the foil and then fold up the ends, making sure to double fold the foil to seal the packet.
5. Bake for 12 to 15 minutes, until the fish is cooked and the vegetables are just tender.
6. To serve, carefully open each foil packet and sprinkle with fresh basil.

Storage Tip: This dish is best eaten immediately. However, you can store leftovers in an airtight container for up to 1 day. Reheat in a 325°F oven, on a baking sheet lined with foil, for about 5 minutes.

Cooking Tip: Be sure to use the same size fish fillets for each packet to ensure even cooking.

Per Serving: Calories: 150; Total fat: 2g; Sodium: 274mg; Carbohydrates: 3g; Fiber: 1g; Sugar: 2g; Protein: 31g

Balsamic-and-Honey-Glazed Salmon

SERVES 4 / PREP TIME: 5 MINUTES / COOK TIME: 20 MINUTES

A delicious pan-seared, balsamic-glazed salmon is rich and hearty. Salmon is a versatile fish that can be paired with so many sides, and it cooks quickly. Enjoy this recipe with Roasted Lemon Asparagus (page 85) or Green Bean and Mushroom Sauté (page 84).

4 tablespoons balsamic vinegar

Juice of 1 large lime

1 teaspoon Dijon mustard

1 teaspoon honey

1 tablespoon olive oil

4 (5-to-6-ounce) salmon fillets

½ teaspoon salt

½ teaspoon freshly ground black pepper

1. In a small saucepan over medium-high heat, mix the balsamic vinegar, lime juice, Dijon mustard, and honey. Bring to a boil. Reduce the heat to medium and let simmer until slightly thick, about 10 minutes. Remove from the heat.

2. In a sauté pan over medium heat, warm the olive oil.

3. Season the salmon fillets with salt and pepper, place them in the pan, and cook on one side for 5 minutes. Turn the salmon and cook the other side for 3 minutes.

4. Serve drizzled with the balsamic-honey glaze.

Storage Tip: This dish is best eaten immediately. However, you can store it in an airtight container in the refrigerator overnight. To reheat, wrap in foil and place in a preheated 350°F oven for 10 minutes.

Per Serving: Calories: 223; Total fat: 9g; Sodium: 326mg; Carbohydrates: 4g; Fiber: 0g; Sugar: 2g; Protein: 29g

Beef and Pork

< Sheet Pan Sirloin Steak, Mushrooms, and Broccoli, page 63

Beef Taco Filling

GLUTEN-FREE / NUT-FREE

SERVES 4 / PREP TIME: 5 MINUTES / COOK TIME: 15 MINUTES

You won't want a drive-through taco again after enjoying one with this wonderful beef filling. Adjust the spice level to your family's preference.

1 teaspoon olive oil

1 onion, diced

2 garlic cloves, finely chopped

1 pound lean ground beef

2 teaspoons Taco Seasoning Mix (page 97)

8 ounces tomato sauce

OPTIONAL TOPPINGS:

Taco shells

Diced tomatoes

Chopped lettuce

Shredded Mexican-style cheese

Sour cream

Salsa

Classic Guacamole (page 76)

1. In a large saucepan over medium heat, warm the olive oil. Add the onion and sauté until softened, about 3 minutes. Add the garlic and sauté another 30 seconds. Add the ground beef and cook, using a wooden spoon to break it up, until cooked through and no longer pink. Drain and discard any fat. Stir in the taco seasoning and the tomato sauce and let simmer until heated through, about 10 minutes.

2. Serve as tacos with taco shells and your choice of optional toppings.

Storage Tip: I recommend making a double batch and freezing half for up to 3 months. You can use the leftovers to make Taco Soup (page 26). To defrost the meat, place the beef in the refrigerator overnight.

Per Serving: Calories: 346; Total fat: 25g; Sodium: 794mg; Carbohydrates: 8g; Fiber: 1g; Sugar: 3g; Protein: 21g

VARIATIONS

Beef Quesadillas

Lay out 4 flour tortillas on a clean work surface. Spoon ¼ cup of the beef taco filling on each tortilla. Sprinkle each with 2 ounces of shredded Mexican-style cheese. Place a tortilla over the cheese. Heat a large skillet over medium heat and warm 1 tablespoon of olive oil. Place one of the quesadillas into the pan and cook for 2 minutes. Carefully flip the quesadilla and cook for another 2 minutes. Repeat with the other 3 quesadillas. Cut into wedges and serve with diced tomatoes, sour cream, and guacamole.

Per Serving: Calories: 770; Total fat: 57g; Sodium: 1,287mg; Carbohydrates: 26g; Fiber: 3g; Sugar: 3g; Protein: 36g

Taco Salad

Cut 1 head of iceberg lettuce into shreds and put it in a large bowl. Add a 16-ounce can of drained and rinsed black beans, 1 cup of shredded Mexican-style cheese, and the beef taco filling. Toss the ingredients together. Drizzle with House Salad Dressing (page 99).

Per Serving (without dressing): Calories: 661; Total fat: 41g; Sodium: 1,147mg; Carbohydrates: 30g; Fiber: 8g; Sugar: 7g; Protein: 41g

Build Your Burger

SERVES 4 / PREP TIME: 10 MINUTES / COOK TIME: 8 TO 10 MINUTES

A tender, juicy burger is one of the most pleasing dinners. You'll find yourself using this recipe all the time. With just a few minutes of prep work, you and your family will be enjoying big, beefy burger flavor. It's the best!

1 pound ground beef

1 teaspoon Seasoned Salt (page 96)

1 teaspoon Dijon mustard

3 dashes Worcestershire sauce

4 hamburger buns

OPTIONAL TOPPINGS:

Homemade Dijonnaise (page 100)

Lettuce

Sliced tomato

Pickles

Ketchup

1. Preheat a grill pan or sauté pan over medium-high heat.

2. In a large bowl, mix the ground beef, seasoned salt, Dijon mustard, and Worcestershire sauce. Form the mixture into 4 equal hamburgers. Press the center of each hamburger to help them cook evenly.

3. Place each hamburger in the pan and cook, undisturbed, for 5 minutes. Flip each burger and cook until they reach your desired doneness, 3 to 5 minutes.

4. Place each burger on the bottom of a hamburger bun, add your favorite toppings, and finish with the top bun. Serve immediately.

Addition Tip: Make a cheeseburger by adding a slice of American cheese to each burger 2 minutes before the burgers are done cooking on the second side. Make a bacon cheeseburger by adding a slice of American cheese and cooked bacon 2 minutes before the burger is finished cooking on the second side.

Per Serving: Calories: 486; Total fat: 33g; Sodium: 539mg; Carbohydrates: 24g; Fiber: 0g; Sugar: 3g; Protein: 23g

Sheet Pan Sirloin Steak, Mushrooms, and Broccoli

SERVES 4 / PREP TIME: 10 MINUTES / COOK TIME: 20 MINUTES

Bring the steakhouse to your table with this easy sheet pan recipe. A tender, juicy steak with mushrooms and broccoli will be a one-pan winner dinner. The beef and veggies make a perfectly seasoned meal that you'll hardly believe could be ready in 30 minutes. Serve with Go-To Chopped Salad (page 30) and Garlic-Roasted Potatoes (page 80).

1 cup halved button mushrooms

2 cups broccoli florets

2 tablespoons olive oil, divided

2 teaspoons Seasoned Salt (page 96), divided

2 pounds sirloin steak

1. Preheat the oven to 425°F. Place the mushrooms and broccoli on a large baking sheet and drizzle 1 tablespoon of olive oil and sprinkle 1 teaspoon of seasoned salt over the vegetables.

2. Roast for 10 minutes.

3. Drizzle the remaining 1 tablespoon of olive oil and sprinkle the remaining 1 teaspoon of seasoned salt on both sides of the sirloin steak. Set aside on a plate.

4. Adjust the oven to broil.

5. Push the vegetables to one side of the baking sheet and place the sirloin steak on the other side. Broil, about 6 inches away from the heat source, up to 5 minutes per side, until cooked to your desired doneness.

Cooking Tips:
- Use a meat thermometer to check the internal temperature of the steaks: Rare: 120–125°F; Medium-rare: 130–140°F; Medium: 140–150°F; Medium-well: 150–160°F; Well-done: 160–170°F.
- Cook the steaks about 5 to 6 inches away from the heat source. A 1-inch-thick steak should be checked after it has been flipped and broiled at least 3 minutes.

Per Serving: Calories: 563; Total fat: 41g; Sodium: 524mg; Carbohydrates: 4g; Fiber: 1g; Sugar: 1g; Protein: 46g

Beef and Pepper Stir-Fry

SERVES 4 / PREP TIME: 10 MINUTES / COOK TIME: 10 MINUTES

If you're looking for some Asian flavors, this stir-fry delivers. Marinating the meat with Brown Sugar–Soy Sauce (page 101) for just a few minutes makes the beef extra tender. I love this dish over steamed rice, cauliflower rice, or Easy Garlic-Parmesan Zoodles (page 82).

1 pound flank steak, thinly sliced

1 cup Brown Sugar–Soy Sauce (page 101), divided

2 red bell peppers, seeded and thinly sliced

1 large onion, thinly sliced

1 teaspoon Ginger-Cinnamon Seasoning Mix (page 97)

1 tablespoon olive oil

OPTIONAL GARNISH:

Sliced green onions

1. In a medium bowl, toss together the steak and ½ cup of the brown sugar–soy sauce and let marinate for a few minutes.

2. In another medium bowl, toss together the bell pepper, onions, and ginger-cinnamon seasoning.

3. Remove the steak from the marinade and pat the meat dry with a paper towel, which will allow it to sear properly.

4. In a large skillet or wok over medium-high heat, warm the olive oil. Add the sliced beef and let cook for 3 minutes. If your pan is not large enough for all the beef, cook it in two batches. Stir in the peppers and onions and let cook another 2 minutes. Pour in the remaining ½ cup of brown sugar–soy sauce, reduce the heat to medium-low, and simmer until cooked through, about 2 minutes.

5. Sprinkle with sliced green onions (if using) and serve hot.

Storage Tip: Leftovers can be kept in an airtight container in the refrigerator for up to 2 days.

Shortcut: Purchase precut stir-fry beef instead of cutting it yourself. You can buy precut frozen peppers and onions as well.

Per Serving: Calories: 260; Total fat: 11g; Sodium: 859mg; Carbohydrates: 15g; Fiber: 2g; Sugar: 7g; Protein: 27g

Garlic Butter Steak and Potatoes

SERVES 4 / PREP TIME: 5 MINUTES / COOK TIME: 20 MINUTES

Here is the ultimate meat and potatoes dinner. It's amazing how a little garlic, butter, and Italian seasoning can deliver an abundance of flavor that is sure to become a family favorite. Pair it with Easy Garlic Crostini (page 77), Roasted Lemon Asparagus (page 85), or the Go-To Chopped Salad (page 30).

1 pound sirloin steak, cut into ½-inch cubes

Salt

Freshly ground black pepper

2 tablespoons olive oil, divided

3 tablespoons butter, divided

1 pound russet or Yukon Gold potatoes, cut into ½-inch rounds

1 teaspoon Italian Herb Seasoning Mix (page 97)

3 garlic cloves, minced

Chopped fresh parsley, for garnish

1. Season the steak with salt and pepper and set aside.
2. In a large sauté pan over medium heat, warm 1 tablespoon of olive oil and 1 tablespoon of butter. Add the potatoes, season with the Italian herb seasoning, and cook, stirring occasionally, until tender, about 10 minutes. Remove the potatoes and set aside.
3. Add the remaining 1 tablespoon of olive oil and 2 tablespoons of butter to the pan and heat until the butter is melted. Add the garlic and cook for 1 minute. Add the steak and cook to your desired doneness, 5 to 7 minutes.
4. Add the potatoes back to the pan to warm. Taste and add salt and pepper if needed. Sprinkle with parsley and serve.

Storage Tip: Leftovers can be stored in an airtight container in the refrigerator for up to 2 days.

Shortcut: Use precut beef that can be purchased at the butcher.

Per Serving: Calories: 460; Total fat: 32g; Sodium: 276mg; Carbohydrates: 19g; Fiber: 3g; Sugar: 1g; Protein: 24g

Pan-Seared Pork Chops and Parmesan Spinach

SERVES 4 / PREP TIME: 5 MINUTES / COOK TIME: 13 MINUTES

Fork-tender pork chops, seasoned perfectly and quickly pan-seared, are on the list of the quickest and most delectable recipes. As the cooked pork rests, the fresh spinach quickly sautés, delivering a mouthwatering dinner. Serve it with Garlic Butter Rice (page 81) or the Go-To Chopped Salad (page 30).

2 tablespoons olive oil, divided

1 tablespoon butter

4 (4-ounce) boneless pork chops

1 tablespoon Seasoned Salt (page 96)

2 garlic cloves, minced

1 pound baby spinach

2 tablespoons grated Parmigiano-Reggiano cheese

Salt

Freshly ground black pepper

OPTIONAL GARNISH:

Chopped fresh parsley

1. In a large sauté pan over medium heat, warm 1 tablespoon of olive oil and the butter.

2. Season the pork chops with the seasoned salt, place them in the hot pan, and cook for 5 minutes. Flip the chops and cook for another 4 to 5 minutes. Transfer the pork to a plate and set aside to rest.

3. Add the remaining 1 tablespoon of olive oil to the pan, add the garlic, and cook, stirring, for 30 seconds.

4. Add the baby spinach and cook, stirring occasionally, until wilted, about 2 minutes. Drain any excess water from pan. Add the Parmigiano-Reggiano cheese. Taste and season with salt and pepper, if needed.

5. Spoon the spinach onto plates and top with a pork chop. Sprinkle with chopped parsley (if using) and serve.

Substitution Tip: Replace the spinach with one of the following: 2 cups of broccoli florets, sautéed for about 4 minutes; 1 cup of sliced zucchini or yellow squash, sautéed for 4 to 5 minutes; or 2 cups of chopped cauliflower, sautéed for about 10 minutes.

Per Serving: Calories: 270; Total fat: 16g; Sodium: 1,293mg; Carbohydrates: 6g; Fiber: 3g; Sugar: 0g; Protein: 25g

Pork Piccata

SERVES 4 / PREP TIME: 5 MINUTES / COOK TIME: 15 MINUTES

Capers provide a tangy flavor that enhances these pork chops, which are topped with a fragrant lemon butter sauce. This dish tastes great with Garlic Butter Rice (page 81) or spaghetti.

4 tablespoons butter

4 boneless pork cutlets, pounded to 1 inch thick

½ teaspoon salt

½ teaspoon freshly ground black pepper

1 cup chicken stock

2 tablespoons lemon juice

¼ cup capers, drained

OPTIONAL GARNISHES:

Lemon wedges

Chopped fresh parsley

1. In a skillet over medium heat, warm the butter.
2. Season the pork with salt and pepper.
3. Place the pork cutlets in the hot pan and cook for 4 minutes per side. Add the chicken stock, lemon juice, and capers. Let simmer for about 5 minutes, until cooked through.
4. Sprinkle the cutlets with parsley and serve with lemon wedges (if using).

Storage Tip: Leftovers can be stored in an airtight container and refrigerated for up to 2 days.

Per Serving: Calories: 249; Total fat: 15g; Sodium: 709mg; Carbohydrates: 1g; Fiber: 0g; Sugar: 0g; Protein: 27g

Herb-Roasted Pork Tenderloin

SERVES 4 / PREP TIME: 5 MINUTES / COOK TIME: 15 TO 20 MINUTES

This is a fabulous, easy dinner after a busy workday. Pair with Garlic Butter Rice (page 81) and Roasted Lemon Asparagus (page 85) for a spectacular meal.

1½ pounds pork tenderloin

1 teaspoon Italian Herb Seasoning Mix (page 97)

1 teaspoon olive oil

1. Preheat the oven to 425°F.
2. Season the pork with the Italian herb seasoning.
3. In an ovenproof skillet over medium heat, sear the pork tenderloin on all sides until golden brown, about 3 minutes.
4. Place the pan in the oven and bake for 10 minutes, until the internal temperature of the tenderloin is 145°F. Let rest 5 minutes before cutting into slices and serving.

Storage Tip: Leftovers can be stored in an airtight container in the refrigerator for up to 2 days. Reheat in a 300°F oven on a baking sheet covered with foil for 10 minutes, until heated through.

Per Serving: Calories: 354; Total fat: 15g; Sodium: 290mg; Carbohydrates: 1g; Fiber: 0g; Sugar: 0g; Protein: 50g

Skillet Sausage and Peppers

SERVES 4 / PREP TIME: 10 MINUTES / COOK TIME: 20 MINUTES

Italian sausages sautéed with fresh red and yellow peppers and onions in marinara sauce make a flavorful dish that is perfect served on Italian bread or a hoagie roll.

1 teaspoon olive oil

1 pound Italian pork sausages

2 bell peppers, red and yellow, seeded and chopped

1 onion, chopped

1 cup marinara sauce

Salt

Freshly ground black pepper

Italian bread or hoagie rolls

OPTIONAL GARNISHES:

Chopped fresh basil

Grated Parmigiano-Reggiano

1. In a large skillet over medium heat, warm the olive oil. Add the pork sausages and cook, turning occasionally, about 10 minutes.

2. Transfer the sausages to a cutting board and cut into ½-inch slices.

3. Add the peppers and onions to the skillet and cook, stirring frequently, until they soften, about 3 minutes. Add the sliced sausages back to the skillet and let cook another 2 minutes. Add the marinara sauce, stir to combine, and let simmer 5 more minutes until heated through. Taste and season with salt and pepper, if needed.

4. Serve on Italian bread or hoagie rolls and top with fresh chopped basil and grated Parmigiano-Reggiano (if using).

Per Serving (without bread): Calories: 358; Total fat: 26g; Sodium: 1,262mg; Carbohydrates: 12g; Fiber: 3g; Sugar: 6g; Protein: 18g

One-Pan Sausage and Cabbage

SERVES 4 / PREP TIME: 5 MINUTES / COOK TIME: 20 MINUTES

Ready for pure comfort food? Tasty smoked sausage pairs with cabbage for an aromatic marriage of flavor and makes for a hearty meal that's ready in no time.

2 teaspoons olive oil, divided

1 pound smoked kielbasa sausage, cut into ½-inch slices

1 large onion, chopped

2 garlic cloves, minced

1 small head of cabbage, cored and chopped

1 teaspoon Cajun Seasoning Mix (page 97)

1. In a skillet over medium heat, warm 1 teaspoon of olive oil. Add the kielbasa and cook, turning to brown all sides, for about 5 minutes. Transfer the kielbasa to a plate and set aside.

2. In the same skillet, add the remaining 1 teaspoon of olive oil. Add the onions and cook, stirring occasionally, for 3 minutes. Add the garlic, cabbage, and Cajun seasoning. Stir to combine.

3. Cover the pan with a lid and let simmer until the cabbage is soft and cooked through, about 10 minutes.

4. Add the kielbasa back to the pan and cook until heated through, about 5 minutes. Serve immediately.

Storage Tip: Leftovers can be stored in an airtight container and refrigerated for up to 2 days. Reheat in a 325°F oven in a casserole dish covered with foil until heated through.

Per Serving: Calories: 363; Total fat: 25g; Sodium: 1,370mg; Carbohydrates: 18g; Fiber: 5g; Sugar: 7g; Protein: 21g

Snacks and Sides

< Roasted Lemon Asparagus, page 85

Basic Deviled Eggs

NUT-FREE

SERVES 8 / PREP TIME: 10 MINUTES / COOK TIME: 12 MINUTES

This classic appetizer makes a great side dish and is a welcome addition to a picnic, but really, you can enjoy these eggs anytime—they're always a hit! And by changing just a few ingredients, you can easily change up the flavors.

4 eggs

2 tablespoons Homemade Dijonnaise (page 100)

½ teaspoon white vinegar

Salt

Freshly ground black pepper

Paprika, for garnish

1. Place the eggs in a saucepan, add enough water to completely cover the eggs, place over medium-high heat, and bring to a boil. Remove the pot from the heat, cover with a lid, and let sit for 12 minutes.
2. Remove the lid and run cold water over the eggs to cool.
3. Peel the eggs and cut them in half lengthwise.
4. Remove the yolks from the eggs and place them in a small bowl. Set the whites aside on a plate.
5. Using a fork, mash together the yolks, Dijonnaise, and white vinegar. Taste and add salt and pepper, if needed.
6. Spoon the egg mixture into the egg whites. Sprinkle the tops with paprika. Cover with plastic wrap and refrigerate for 10 to 15 minutes before serving.

Storage Tip: Deviled eggs can be stored in an airtight container in the refrigerator for up to 2 days. Be sure to use a container that's large enough that it won't smash the tops of the eggs.

Shortcut: You can hard-boil the eggs up to 5 days ahead of time and store them in the refrigerator until you are ready to make the deviled eggs.

Per Serving: Calories: 73; Total fat: 6g; Sodium: 83mg; Carbohydrates: <1g; Fiber: 0g; Sugar: 1g; Protein: 3g

VARIATIONS

Buffalo Deviled Eggs

When mashing the yolks, instead of Dijonnaise, add 2½ tablespoons of mayonnaise, 2 tablespoons of hot sauce, and 1 finely chopped celery stalk along with the vinegar. Mix, then taste and add salt and freshly ground black pepper, if needed. Continue with the recipe as instructed and garnish with 2 teaspoons of crumbled blue cheese.

Per Serving: Calories: 71; Total fat: 6g; Sodium: 135mg; Carbohydrates: <1g; Fiber: 0g; Sugar: 1g; Protein: 3g

Horseradish Deviled Eggs

When mashing the yolks, Dijonnaise, and vinegar, add ¾ teaspoon of prepared horseradish. Mix, then taste and add salt and freshly ground black pepper, if needed. Continue with the recipe as instructed.

Per Serving: Calories: 73; Total fat: 6g; Sodium: 85mg; Carbohydrates: <1g; Fiber: 0g; Sugar: 1g; Protein: 3g

Basil Pesto Deviled Eggs

When mashing the yolks, Dijonnaise, and vinegar, add 1 teaspoon of Nut-Free Basil Pesto (page 98) or store-bought pesto. Mix, then taste and add salt and freshly ground black pepper, if needed. Continue with the recipe as instructed.

Per Serving: Calories: 75; Total fat: 7g; Sodium: 88mg; Carbohydrates: <1g; Fiber: 0g; Sugar: 1g; Protein: 3g

Bacon Deviled Eggs

When mashing the yolks, Dijonnaise, and vinegar, add 2 slices of cooked and crumbled bacon. Mix, then taste and add salt and freshly ground black pepper, if needed. Continue with the recipe as instructed.

Per Serving: Calories: 84; Total fat: 7g; Sodium: 124mg; Carbohydrates: <1g; Fiber: 0g; Sugar: 1g; Protein: 4g

Cajun Deviled Eggs

When mashing the yolks, instead of Dijonnaise, add 2½ tablespoons of mayonnaise, 1 teaspoon of Dijon mustard, and 1 teaspoon of Cajun Seasoning Mix (page 97) along with the vinegar. Mix, then taste and add salt and freshly ground black pepper, if needed. Continue with the recipe as instructed.

Per Serving: Calories: 66; Total fat: 6g; Sodium: 171mg; Carbohydrates: 1g; Fiber: 0g; Sugar: 1g; Protein: 3g

Classic Guacamole

SERVES 4 / PREP TIME: 10 MINUTES

There is nothing better than a bowl of fresh guacamole with the zesty tang of lime juice and a hint of spice. It is so easy to make your own guacamole that, honestly, I don't know why anyone buys it. It pairs perfectly with the Beef Taco Filling (page 60), Sheet Pan Nachos (page 78), or with your favorite tortilla chips.

2 teaspoons lime juice

½ red onion, diced

2 garlic cloves, minced

2 ripe avocadoes, pitted and peeled

½ teaspoon ground cumin

½ teaspoon salt

½ teaspoon freshly ground black pepper

OPTIONAL GARNISH:

Chopped fresh cilantro

1. In a small bowl, mix the lime juice, red onion, and minced garlic.
2. In another bowl, using a fork, mash the avocadoes, leaving a few chunks of avocado for texture. Add the cumin, salt, pepper, and the onion mixture. Blend well. Taste and add salt and pepper, if needed.
3. Spoon into a bowl and sprinkle with chopped cilantro (if using). Serve immediately.

Storage Tip: Guacamole is best served immediately; however, leftovers can be stored in an airtight container in the refrigerator overnight. Add a small amount of water over the guacamole to prevent browning before sealing the lid. Drain the water before serving.

Addition Tip: Mix in 1 diced plum tomato for a heartier guacamole.

Per Serving: Calories: 153; Total fat: 13g; Sodium: 298mg; Carbohydrates: 9g; Fiber: 6g; Sugar: 1g; Protein: 2g

Easy Garlic Crostini

SERVES 4 / PREP TIME: 5 MINUTES / COOK TIME: 1 MINUTE

One of my favorite ways to use fresh or leftover bread is to make crispy, crunchy crostini. Topped with Nut-Free Basil Pesto (page 98) or Classic Guacamole (page 76), this is a wonderful accompaniment to soups and salads.

1 loaf Italian bread

2 tablespoons olive oil

1 garlic clove, cut in half

½ teaspoon kosher salt

1. Preheat the oven to broil. Have a baking sheet ready.

2. Cut the bread into ¼-inch slices. Brush the olive oil onto the sliced bread. Rub the garlic over each slice, sprinkle with salt, and place on the baking sheet in a single layer.

3. Place the baking sheet in the oven, 5 to 6 inches from the heat, and broil for 1 minute, until toasted. Watch carefully to make sure the slices don't burn.

Storage Tip: Crostini can be stored in a plastic storage bag at room temperature for up to 5 days. To reheat, wrap the crostini in aluminum foil, place on a baking sheet, and heat in a 320°F oven for about 5 minutes until heated through.

Per Serving: Calories: 330; Total fat: 11g; Sodium: 870mg; Carbohydrates: 50g; Fiber: 3g; Sugar: 3g; Protein: 9g

Sheet Pan Nachos

SERVES 4 / PREP TIME: 5 MINUTES / COOK TIME: 6 MINUTES

Nachos make any meal or snack time festive and fun, and they are really easy to make. Tortilla chips are loaded with zesty Beef Taco Filling (page 60) and topped with black beans and melted cheese. This is best eaten immediately, since the tortilla chips will get soggy if refrigerated with toppings.

1 (14-ounce) bag corn tortilla chips

Beef Taco Filling (page 60)

1 (15-ounce) can black beans, drained and rinsed

¾ cup shredded Cheddar cheese

¾ cup shredded Colby jack cheese

OPTIONAL TOPPINGS:

Classic Guacamole (page 76)

Diced tomatoes

Sour cream

Sliced jalapeños

Diced red onion

Chopped fresh cilantro

1. Preheat the oven to 400°F.
2. Arrange the tortilla chips on a large baking sheet. Spoon the beef taco filling over the tortilla chips and top with black beans. Sprinkle with the shredded cheeses.
3. Bake for 5 to 6 minutes, until the heated through and the cheese is melted. Add optional toppings (if using) or place the toppings in individual bowls and let diners personalize their own nachos.

Substitution Tip: To make a gluten-free recipe, check the package of tortilla chips to be sure they are gluten-free. If you don't want to use tortilla chips, replace them with a 12-ounce bag of frozen tater tots. Bake the tots according to the package instructions, add the beef taco filling and other ingredients, and bake as instructed.

Per Serving: Calories: 1,062; Total fat: 60g; Sodium: 1,593mg; Carbohydrates: 89g; Fiber: 12g; Sugar: 5g; Protein: 44g

Turkey and Cheese Sliders

MAKES 12 SLIDERS / PREP TIME: 10 MINUTES / COOK TIME: 10 MINUTES

Want a quick snack while watching your favorite movie or football game? I've got you covered with these delightful treats.

1 (12-count) package slider buns, each cut in half

1 tablespoon Homemade Dijonnaise (page 100)

1 pound deli-sliced turkey breast

1 cup shredded Italian-blend cheese

½ cup melted butter

Nonstick cooking spray

Poppy seeds, for garnish

1. Preheat the oven to 350°F. Spray a 9-by-13-inch baking dish with nonstick spray.

2. Place the bottoms of the slider rolls in the prepared baking dish.

3. Spread the Dijonnaise over the cut side of the bottom roll. Add layers of turkey and cheese to each bottom. Place the top buns over the cheese. Drizzle the melted butter over the rolls.

4. Cover the baking dish with aluminum foil and bake for 10 minutes, until heated through and the cheese is melted. Serve immediately.

Substitution Tip: Swap the turkey with your favorite deli meat, such as ham or roast beef. Swiss and Cheddar work well in place of Italian-blend cheese.

Per Serving (1 slider): Calories: 250; Total fat: 14g; Sodium: 654mg; Carbohydrates: 21g; Fiber: 1g; Sugar: 5g; Protein: 12g

Garlic-Roasted Potatoes

SERVES 4 / PREP TIME: 5 MINUTES / COOK TIME: 25 MINUTES

Crispy oven-roasted potatoes are crunchy, delicious, and full of flavor, and they go with practically everything. Try them with Build Your Burger (page 62) or Pan-Seared Pork Chops and Parmesan Spinach (page 66).

Nonstick cooking spray

1 pound russet potatoes, scrubbed and cut into 1-inch pieces

1 tablespoon olive oil

1 tablespoon Seasoned Salt (page 96)

1 teaspoon dried parsley

1. Preheat the oven to 425°F. Spray a baking sheet with nonstick cooking spray.
2. Place the potatoes on the baking sheet and drizzle with the olive oil. Sprinkle the potatoes with seasoned salt and parsley and toss to combine.
3. Bake for 15 minutes. Turn the potatoes and bake another 10 minutes, until cooked through and crispy. Serve immediately.

Storage Tip: Roasted potatoes can be stored in an airtight container and refrigerated for up to 3 days or frozen for up to 3 months. To reheat, defrost in the refrigerator overnight, then bake in a 375°F oven for 10 minutes until heated through.

Substitution Tip: Any of the Seasoned Salt variations can be used instead of the Seasoned Salt. Use the same amount and follow the recipe as instructed. Feel free to use avocado, grapeseed, or coconut oil instead of the olive oil.

Per Serving: Calories: 115; Total fat: 4g; Sodium: 609mg; Carbohydrates: 19g; Fiber: 3g; Sugar: 1g; Protein: 2g

Garlic Butter Rice

SERVES 4 / PREP TIME: 5 MINUTES / COOK TIME: 13 MINUTES

This is one of my all-time, favorite, easy recipes. I love the garlic-infused, buttery rice. Pair it with Easy Baked Chicken Breasts (page 48) or Pork Piccata (page 67).

1 teaspoon olive oil

4 tablespoons butter, divided

2 garlic cloves, minced

1 cup white rice

1 cup chicken broth

2 green onions, diced

1. In a large saucepan over medium heat, warm the olive oil and 2 tablespoons of butter. Add the garlic and sauté for 1 minute. Add the rice and cook, stirring occasionally, for 2 minutes. Add the chicken broth, stir, and cover with a lid. Reduce the heat to low and simmer until the liquid is absorbed and the rice is tender, about 10 minutes.

2. Remove the pot from heat and let rest with the cover on for 5 minutes.

3. Add the remaining 2 tablespoons of butter and the green onion and stir to combine. Taste and season with salt and pepper, if needed. Serve warm.

Storage Tip: Rice is best eaten right away; however, leftovers can be stored in an airtight container and refrigerated for up to 2 days. To reheat, place the rice and a little bit of water in a small saucepan over medium heat and cook, stirring frequently, until the rice is warmed through, about 5 minutes. It can also be microwaved in a microwave-safe bowl at medium power for about 2 minutes.

Addition Tip: Add ½ cup of chopped fresh basil or parsley or 2 teaspoons of dried basil or parsley. Also try ¼ cup of chopped fresh cilantro or 1 teaspoon of dried cilantro. Stir the herbs in at the end, just before serving.

Per Serving: Calories: 287; Total fat: 13g; Sodium: 244mg; Carbohydrates: 38g; Fiber: 1g; Sugar: <1g; Protein: 4g

Easy Garlic-Parmesan Zoodles

SERVES 4 / PREP TIME: 5 MINUTES / COOK TIME: 5 MINUTES

For those few people who haven't heard of zoodles, they are spiralized zucchini, and they are a wonderful replacement for spaghetti and other types of pasta. What makes them even better is that they are ready in no time and can be topped with so many sauces, like Nut-Free Basil Pesto (page 98) or your favorite marinara sauce. They're great paired with Pork Piccata (page 67) or Seared Sea Scallops (page 55).

2 large zucchini, trimmed

1 tablespoon olive oil

2 garlic cloves, minced

1 teaspoon grated Parmigiano-Reggiano cheese

Salt

Freshly ground black pepper

1. Place the zucchini in a spiralizer to cut the noodles. Set aside.
2. In a large skillet over medium heat, warm the olive oil. Add the garlic and sauté a few seconds. Add the zoodles and sauté until tender, about 5 minutes.
3. Add the Parmigiano-Reggiano and season with salt and pepper to taste.

Storage Tip: Leftovers can be stored in an airtight container in the refrigerator for up to 2 days. Reheat in a saucepan sprayed with nonstick cooking spray and cook for about 2 minutes until heated through.

Shortcut: You can purchase pre-spiralized zoodles in the produce section of your grocery store.

Per Serving: Calories: 60; Total fat: 4g; Sodium: 19mg; Carbohydrates: 6g; Fiber: 2g; Sugar: 3g; Protein: 2g

VARIATION

Sweet-Savory Zoodles

Instead of the Parmigiano-Reggiano cheese, add 2 tablespoons of Brown Sugar–Soy Sauce (page 101) to the zoodles after they have cooked for about 3 minutes. Sauté another 1 to 2 minutes and serve.

Per Serving: Calories: 62; Total fat: 4g; Sodium: 91mg; Carbohydrates: 7g; Fiber: 2g; Sugar: 3g; Protein: 2g

Green Bean and Mushroom Sauté

SERVES 4 / PREP TIME: 10 MINUTES / COOK TIME: 10 MINUTES

Green beans and mushrooms make for a delicious, healthy, low-carb side dish that's ready in 20 minutes. I love this recipe because it can be made ahead and reheated. It's a perfect side dish for any night, but it's special enough for a holiday, too! Pair with Herb-Roasted Pork Tenderloin (page 68) or Baked Parmesan Chicken Tenders (page 50).

1 teaspoon salt, plus more
if needed

**1 pound fresh green
beans, trimmed**

Large bowl of ice water

2 tablespoons butter

1 small shallot, diced

**8 ounces mushrooms,
thinly sliced**

Freshly ground black pepper

1. In a medium pot over medium-high heat, bring 3 cups of water and the salt to a boil. Add the green beans, reduce the heat to medium-low, and cook for 3 minutes. Drain the beans and immediately transfer them to the bowl of ice water. This will stop the cooking and preserve the bright green color of the beans.

2. In the same pot over medium heat, melt the butter. Add the shallots and sauté until softened, about 2 minutes. Stir in the mushrooms and cook, stirring occasionally, until tender, 2 to 3 minutes.

3. Add the beans back into the pan with the mushrooms and cook until heated through. Season with salt and pepper, if needed. Serve warm.

Storage Tip: Leftovers can be stored in an airtight container and refrigerated for up to 3 days. To reheat, place the beans and mushrooms in an oven-safe casserole dish in a 325°F oven for 15 minutes until heated through.

Shortcut: Presliced mushrooms are sold in the produce section of your local grocer.

Per Serving: Calories: 102; Total fat: 6g; Sodium: 592mg; Carbohydrates: 11g; Fiber: 5g; Sugar: 5g; Protein: 4g

Roasted Lemon Asparagus

SERVES 4 / PREP TIME: 5 MINUTES / COOK TIME: 10 TO 15 MINUTES

Tender asparagus loaded with lemon and garlic makes a great side dish any night of the week, but especially for dinner parties. This elegant and delicious dish requires little work for a big payoff. Pair with Pan-Seared Pork Chops and Parmesan Spinach (page 66) or Easy Baked Chicken Breasts (page 48).

1 pound fresh asparagus, trimmed

1 tablespoon olive oil

1 lemon, ½ juiced and ½ thinly sliced

1 garlic clove, minced

½ teaspoon salt

¼ teaspoon freshly ground black pepper

1. Preheat the oven to 425°F.
2. Arrange the asparagus on a large baking sheet. Drizzle with the olive oil and lemon juice. Arrange the lemon slices over the asparagus. Scatter the garlic over the asparagus and season with salt and pepper.
3. Roast for 10 to 15 minutes, until the asparagus are tender. Serve warm

Storage Tip: Leftovers can be stored in an airtight container and refrigerated for up to 3 days. Reheat in a saucepan over medium heat, add a drizzle of olive oil, and cook for 3 minutes until heated through.

Cooking Tip: Thicker asparagus will take longer to roast. Check them for doneness at around 12 minutes.

Per Serving: Calories: 63; Total fat: 4g; Sodium: 294mg; Carbohydrates: 8g; Fiber: 4g; Sugar: 2g; Protein: 3g

Desserts

< Chocolate-Dipped Ice Cream Sandwiches, page 93

Mini Cheesecakes

MAKES 6 MINI CHEESECAKES / PREP TIME: 10 MINUTES / COOK TIME: 15 TO 20 MINUTES

I think mini cheesecakes with a vanilla wafer crust and a luscious creamy filling are the perfect dessert. Since they're made in muffin tins, these bake up easy, and they are adorable.

6 vanilla wafers

8 ounces cream cheese

¼ cup sugar

½ teaspoon vanilla extract

1 egg

OPTIONAL TOPPINGS:

Fruit preserves, such as strawberry, raspberry, or blueberry

Sliced fruit, such as strawberries or blueberries

1. Preheat the oven to 350°F. Line a 6-cup muffin tin with cupcake liners.
2. Place a vanilla wafer in the bottom of each liner.
3. In medium bowl, using a hand mixer, beat the cream cheese, sugar, vanilla, and egg until smooth.
4. Pour the mixture into each muffin cup, filling each cup about three-quarters full.
5. Bake for 15 minutes. The center of the cheesecake should be set but slightly jiggly. If needed, bake for another 5 minutes. Let cool slightly and top with fruit preserves or sliced fruit (if using) before serving.

Per Serving: Calories: 203; Total fat: 15g; Sodium: 142mg; Carbohydrates: 14g; Fiber: 0g; Sugar: 12g; Protein: 4g

VARIATIONS

Mini Lemon Cheesecakes
Replace the vanilla extract with ½ teaspoon of lemon extract and follow the recipe instructions. Top with fresh blueberries.
Per Serving: Calories: 203; Total fat: 15g; Sodium: 142mg; Carbohydrates: 14g; Fiber: 0g; Sugar: 12g; Protein: 4g

Mini Almond Cheesecakes
Replace the vanilla extract with ½ teaspoon of almond extract and follow the recipe instructions.
Per Serving: Calories: 203; Total fat: 15g; Sodium: 142mg; Carbohydrates: 14g; Fiber: 0g; Sugar: 12g; Protein: 4g

Mini Chocolate Cheesecakes
Add 1 teaspoon of unsweetened cocoa powder to the cream cheese, sugar, vanilla, and egg. Beat with a hand mixer and continue following the recipe instructions.
Per Serving: Calories: 203; Total fat: 15g; Sodium: 142mg; Carbohydrates: 14g; Fiber: 0g; Sugar: 12g; Protein: 4g

Roasted Maple-Cinnamon Bananas and Walnuts

SERVES 4 / PREP TIME: 5 MINUTES / COOK TIME: 15 MINUTES

As the bananas roast, they caramelize and become even more sweet from the maple syrup, making this a truly marvelous dessert. Chopped walnuts add a nice crunch. Top with a scoop of vanilla ice cream.

Nonstick cooking spray

4 bananas, cut in half lengthwise

1 tablespoon pure maple syrup

1 teaspoon ground cinnamon

2 teaspoons chopped walnuts

1. Preheat the oven to 375°F. Spray a casserole dish with nonstick cooking spray.
2. Place the bananas, cut-side down, in the casserole dish. Drizzle the maple syrup over the bananas and sprinkle with the cinnamon.
3. Cover the casserole dish with aluminum foil and bake for 15 minutes.
4. Sprinkle with chopped walnuts and serve warm.

Storage Tip: The baked bananas are best eaten right after you make them.

Cooking Tip: Be sure to use pure maple syrup, not pancake syrup. If maple syrup is unavailable, honey can be used instead.

Per Serving: Calories: 128; Total fat: 1g; Sodium: 2mg; Carbohydrates: 31g; Fiber: 4g; Sugar: 18g; Protein: 1g

Warm Apple Foldovers

NUT-FREE

MAKES 5 FOLDOVERS / PREP TIME: 10 MINUTES / COOK TIME: 15 MINUTES

Flaky hand pies stuffed with apples and cinnamon and topped with a buttery cinnamon coating make for a delectable dessert. I think Golden Delicious or Granny Smith apples are best in this recipe.

1 (16-ounce) can refrigerated flaky biscuits

¾ cup peeled and chopped apples

⅓ cup sugar

½ teaspoon ground cinnamon

2 tablespoons melted butter

1. Preheat the oven to 375°F. Have a baking sheet ready.
2. Separate the biscuit dough and press into 5 (4-inch) circles. Spoon the apples equally onto one half of each dough circle.
3. In a small bowl, combine the sugar and cinnamon.
4. Sprinkle ½ teaspoon of the cinnamon-sugar mixture over each of the chopped apple and dough circles.
5. Fold each piece of dough in half over the filling and use a fork to seal the edges of the dough.
6. Dip the foldovers into the melted butter and then into the remaining cinnamon-sugar mixture. Place the foldovers on the baking sheet.
7. Bake for 15 to 20 minutes, until the crust is golden brown. Serve warm or cold.

Storage Tip: Foldovers can be stored in an airtight container and refrigerated for up to 3 days. To freeze, place the foldovers on a baking sheet and freeze for 1 hour. This ensures the foldovers will not stick together. Place the foldovers in a freezer-safe storage bag for up to 2 months. To reheat, defrost overnight in the refrigerator. Place the foldovers on a baking sheet and bake in a 325°F oven for 10 minutes.

Variation Tip: Use ¾ cup of chopped pears instead of apples and follow the recipe instructions.

Per Serving: Calories: 271; Total fat: 12g; Sodium: 581mg; Carbohydrates: 40g; Fiber: 2g; Sugar: 19g; Protein: 3g

Chocolate Chip Cookies

MAKES 24 COOKIES / PREP TIME: 10 MINUTES / COOK TIME: 10 MINUTES

These no-fuss, decadent cookies are baked in just minutes! Mix it up by using white chocolate chips or toffee bits instead of the chocolate chips.

4 tablespoons butter

12 ounces chocolate chips

1 (14-ounce) can sweetened condensed milk

1 cup chopped pistachios or walnuts

1 cup all-purpose flour

1. Preheat the oven to 350°F. Have a baking sheet ready.

2. In a small saucepan over medium heat, melt the butter and chocolate chips. Add the sweetened condensed milk and stir to combine. Remove pan from heat. Add the nuts and flour and stir to combine.

3. Drop teaspoons of dough onto the baking sheet and bake for 10 minutes. Transfer to a wire rack to cool slightly and serve.

Storage Tip: These cookies can be stored in an airtight container and refrigerated for up to 4 days.

Per Serving: Calories: 185; Total fat: 11g; Sodium: 46mg; Carbohydrates: 22g; Fiber: 2g; Sugar: 16g; Protein: 3g

Chocolate-Dipped Ice Cream Sandwiches

SERVES 4 / PREP TIME: 10 MINUTES / COOK TIME: 0 MINUTES

Everyone loves an ice cream sandwich! And you can make them at home using your favorite store-bought chocolate chip cookies and ice cream. You can use any flavor of ice cream you like.

4 ounces semisweet chocolate

4 scoops vanilla ice cream

8 chocolate chip cookies (page 92)

OPTIONAL TOPPING:

Rainbow sprinkles

1. Have a baking sheet ready.
2. Place the chocolate in a microwave-safe bowl and microwave for 30 seconds or until melted.
3. Place 1 scoop of ice cream between 2 chocolate chip cookies.
4. Quickly dip the ice cream sandwich into the melted chocolate, coating half of the cookie, then dip the chocolate-covered side into the rainbow sprinkles (if using). Place the ice cream sandwich on a baking sheet. Repeat with the remaining cookies and ice cream.
5. Place the tray in the freezer for about 5 minutes to firm up the chocolate. Serve.

Per Serving: Calories: 638; Total fat: 38g; Sodium: 155mg; Carbohydrates: 77g; Fiber: 7g; Sugar: 59g; Protein: 10g

Spice Blends, Sauces, and Dressings

< Seasoned Salt, page 96

Seasoned Salt

MAKES 1 CUP / PREP TIME: 5 MINUTES

Making your own seasoned salt is cost-effective, and seasoned salts are terrific flavor enhancers in many recipes. This is one of my favorites. I keep a bowl of it on the kitchen counter because I use it on everything. You'll see this recipe called for throughout the book, including in the Garlic-Roasted Potatoes (page 80) and Build Your Burger (page 62) recipes. The variations are great, too, so don't overlook them!

¼ cup salt

¼ cup onion powder

¼ cup garlic powder

2 tablespoons freshly ground black pepper

2 tablespoons dried parsley

2 tablespoons paprika

1. In a small bowl, mix the salt, onion powder, garlic powder, pepper, dried parsley, and paprika.
2. Store in a covered jar or plastic container at room temperature for up to 6 months.

Per Serving (1 teaspoon): Calories: 8; Total fat: <1g; Sodium: 787mg; Carbohydrates: 2g; Fiber: <1g; Sugar: <1g; Protein: <1g

VARIATIONS

Taco Seasoning Mix

Do not use the parsley or paprika. Instead, in a small bowl, mix the salt, onion powder, garlic powder, freshly ground black pepper, 2 tablespoons of ground cumin, and 2 teaspoons of chili powder. Continue following the recipe instructions.

Per Serving (1 teaspoon): Calories: 8; Total fat: <1g; Sodium: 789mg; Carbohydrates: 2g; Fiber: <1g; Sugar: <1g; Protein: <1g

Italian Herb Seasoning Mix

Do not use the parsley or paprika. Instead, in a small bowl, mix the salt, onion powder, garlic powder, freshly ground black pepper, 2 tablespoons of dried basil, and 2 tablespoons of dried oregano. Continue following the recipe instructions.

Per Serving (1 teaspoon): Calories: 8; Total fat: <1g; Sodium: 787mg; Carbohydrates: 2g; Fiber: <11g; Sugar: <1g; Protein: <1g

Ginger-Cinnamon Seasoning Mix

Do not use the parsley or paprika. Instead, in a small bowl, mix the salt, onion powder, garlic powder, freshly ground black pepper, 1 teaspoon of ground ginger, and 1 teaspoon of ground cinnamon. Continue following the recipe instructions.

Per Serving (1 teaspoon): Calories: 7; Total fat: 0g; Sodium: 787mg; Carbohydrates: 2g; Fiber: <1g; Sugar: <1g; Protein: <1g

Cajun Seasoning Mix

Do not use the parsley or paprika. Instead, in a small bowl, mix the salt, onion powder, garlic powder, freshly ground black pepper, 2 tablespoons of smoked paprika, 2 tablespoons of cayenne pepper, and 1 teaspoon of dried oregano. Continue following the recipe instructions.

Per Serving (1 teaspoon): Calories: 9; Total fat: <1g; Sodium: 787mg; Carbohydrates: 2g; Fiber: 1g; Sugar: <1g; Protein: <1g

Nut-Free Basil Pesto

GLUTEN-FREE / NO-COOK / NUT-FREE

MAKES 1 CUP / PREP TIME: 5 MINUTES

This is the go-to pesto that I've been making for years. I usually have some frozen in my freezer, ready to use in a quick and easy dinner. Since store-bought pesto is pretty expensive, this is one of the most cost-effective recipes ever!

2 cups packed fresh basil

½ cup freshly grated Pecorino-Romano cheese

2 garlic cloves, chopped

¼ cup olive oil, plus more if needed

½ teaspoon salt

½ teaspoon freshly ground black pepper

1. In a food processor, combine the basil, Pecorino-Romano cheese, and garlic. Pulse until coarsely chopped.

2. With the processor running, slowly add the olive oil and continue to process until the mixture is emulsified. Scrape down the sides of the bowl with a rubber spatula and, if necessary, continue to process and add a little oil until it reaches your desired consistency. Taste and season with salt and pepper, if needed.

Storage Tip: The pesto can be stored in an airtight container and refrigerated for up to 3 days. To freeze, place 2 tablespoons of the pesto in each cube of an ice cube tray. After the pesto has frozen, transfer the cubes to a freezer-safe storage bag and use when needed. To defrost, place in the refrigerator overnight, then warm in a saucepan.

Per Serving (1 tablespoon): Calories: 42; Total fat: 4g; Sodium: 118mg; Carbohydrates: <1g; Fiber: <1g; Sugar: 0g; Protein: 1g

House Salad Dressing

MAKES 1 CUP / PREP TIME: 5 MINUTES

If you haven't made your own dressing, you've been missing out. This recipe makes a great base, and as you get more comfortable making it, you'll find it easy to experiment by adding fresh herbs such as basil and thyme. Once you make your own dressing, you won't want to buy it ever again.

¼ **cup red wine vinegar**

⅔ cup olive oil

1 teaspoon honey

1 teaspoon Dijon mustard

1 garlic clove, minced

½ teaspoon salt

½ teaspoon freshly ground black pepper

1. In a small bowl, whisk together the vinegar, olive oil, honey, Dijon mustard, minced garlic, salt, and pepper. Taste and adjust the seasonings, if needed.
2. Store in an airtight container in the refrigerator for up to 1 week.

Variation Tip: Lemony House Dressing: Replace the red wine vinegar with ⅓ cup of lemon juice (the juice of about 2 large lemons). Continue following recipe instructions.

Per Serving (1 tablespoon): Calories: 81; Total fat: 9g; Sodium: 80mg; Carbohydrates: 1g; Fiber: 0g; Sugar: <1g; Protein: 0g

Homemade Dijonnaise

MAKES 1 CUP / PREP TIME: 5 MINUTES

I'm always happy when I bite into a sandwich with an unexpected zing. This mayonnaise-based dressing is loaded with flavor and uses just a few simple ingredients. Worcestershire sauce gives a nice pop of flavor to this tasty condiment. Try this with Build Your Burger (page 62) and Creamy Macaroni and Broccoli Salad (page 32).

1 cup mayonnaise

2 tablespoons Dijon mustard

2 to 3 dashes Worcestershire sauce

Salt

Freshly ground black pepper

In a small bowl, mix the mayonnaise, Dijon mustard, and Worcestershire sauce. Add salt and pepper to taste.

Storage Tip: Store in an airtight container in the refrigerator for up to 2 weeks.

Substitution Tip: For a gluten-free recipe, be sure to check the Worcestershire sauce label because not all brands are gluten-free.

Per Serving (1 tablespoon): Calories: 147; Total fat: 16g; Sodium: 190mg; Carbohydrates: <1g; Fiber: 0g; Sugar: 2g; Protein: <1g

Brown Sugar–Soy Sauce

MAKES 1 CUP / PREP TIME: 5 MINUTES

This is one of my favorite sauces to make. It's ready in no time and you can use it in all kinds of recipes. Start by using it in the Turkey Lettuce Wraps (page 52).

2 garlic cloves, minced

2 tablespoons soy sauce

1½ tablespoons brown sugar

1 cup beef broth

1 teaspoon cornstarch

In a small bowl, mix the garlic, soy sauce, brown sugar, beef broth, and cornstarch.

Storage Tip: The sauce can be stored in an airtight container in the refrigerator for up to 1 week.

Per Serving (½ cup): Calories: 56; Total fat: 0g; Sodium: 1,190mg; Carbohydrates: 14g; Fiber: <1g; Sugar: 7g; Protein: 3g

Measurement Conversions

VOLUME EQUIVALENTS (LIQUID)

US STANDARD	US STANDARD (OUNCES)	METRIC (APPROXIMATE)
2 tablespoons	1 fl. oz.	30 mL
¼ cup	2 fl. oz.	60 mL
½ cup	4 fl. oz.	120 mL
1 cup	8 fl. oz.	240 mL
1½ cups	12 fl. oz.	355 mL
2 cups or 1 pint	16 fl. oz.	475 mL
4 cups or 1 quart	32 fl. oz.	1 L
1 gallon	128 fl. oz.	4 L

OVEN TEMPERATURES

FAHRENHEIT	CELSIUS (APPROXIMATE)
250°F	120°C
300°F	150°C
325°F	165°C
350°F	180°C
375°F	190°C
400°F	200°C
425°F	220°C
450°F	230°C

VOLUME EQUIVALENTS (DRY)

US STANDARD	METRIC (APPROXIMATE)
⅛ teaspoon	0.5 mL
¼ teaspoon	1 mL
½ teaspoon	2 mL
¾ teaspoon	4 mL
1 teaspoon	5 mL
1 tablespoon	15 mL
¼ cup	59 mL
⅓ cup	79 mL
½ cup	118 mL
⅔ cup	156 mL
¾ cup	177 mL
1 cup	235 mL
2 cups or 1 pint	475 mL
3 cups	700 mL
4 cups or 1 quart	1 L

WEIGHT EQUIVALENTS

US STANDARD	METRIC (APPROXIMATE)
½ ounce	15 g
1 ounce	30 g
2 ounces	60 g
4 ounces	115 g
8 ounces	225 g
12 ounces	340 g
16 ounces or 1 pound	455 g

Index

Acknowledgments

This is in no particular order, but please know you are all amazing.

Matthew, without your support and love I would never have started a food blog and written a cookbook. You are the best hubs ever. Thank you for your unconditional love.

Mom and Dad, thank you for letting me take over the kitchen when I was a young girl. That freedom has allowed me to enjoy what I love to do every day: create new recipes.

Aidan, thank you for being my sous-chef and co-creator in the kitchen; you are blessed with an amazing palate. You have been testing my creations since you were a baby when I made homemade baby foods. P.S. I cannot thank you enough for all of your cleanup duty.

Mairead, thank you for inspiring me to write this book, especially for those who need quick, easy, and tasty recipes. You are always willing to try new flavors and help me with cleanup.

Sweet Deirdre, love you to the moon and back. Your amazing baking and cooking skills always push me to be a better baker and cook. In addition, you are my social media guru, and you keep me informed always.

Matt, thank you for loving everything I make and always being willing to try some of my crazier ideas.

To one of the nicest and classiest ladies around, my MIL, Dottie, a fantastic cook who has always shared recipes with me. You were the first reader of my food blog. Thank you for always being such a great support.

Lastly, to Laura Apperson and the Callisto Media team, thank you for being such an amazing group. My heart is full of gratitude for all your support.

About the Author

Eileen Kelly is the creator and owner of the food blog
Everyday Eileen (EverydayEileen.com). Her recipes focus
on quick and easy, seasonal recipes that are family
tested and approved, and she creates healthy recipes
with the occasional indulgence. Follow along with
her latest creations on Facebook, Pinterest, Instagram,
and Twitter at @everyday_eileen.

CPSIA information can be obtained
at www.ICGtesting.com
Printed in the USA
BVHW050336280520
580327BV00012B/62

9 781646 119073